# BEYOND
## ANGER

LARRY YEAGLEY

REVIEW AND HERALD® PUBLISHING ASSOCIATION
HAGERSTOWN, MD 21741-1119

The Review and Herald Publishing Association publishes biblically-based materials for
spiritual, physical, and mental growth and Christian discipleship.

The author assumes full responsibility for the accuracy of all facts and quotations as cited
in this book.

Unless otherwise credited, Scripture quotations are from the *New American
Standard Bible,* © The Lockman Foundation 1960, 1962, 1963, 1968, 1971, 1972,
1973, 1975, 1977, 1995.

Texts credited to Message are from *The Message.* Copyright © 1993, 1994, 1995,
1996, 2000, 2001, 2002.
Scripture quotations marked NLT are taken from the *Holy Bible,* New Living
Translation, copyright © 1996. Used by permission of Tyndale House Publishers, Inc.,
Wheaton, Illinois 60189. All rights reserved.
Bible texts credited to TEV are from the *Good News Bible*—Old Testament:
Copyright © American Bible Society 1976, 1992; New Testament: Copyright ©
American Bible Society 1966, 1971, 1976, 1992.
Verses marked TLB are taken from *The Living Bible,* copyright © 1971 by Tyndale
House Publishers, Wheaton, Ill. Used by permission.

This book was
Edited by Gerald Wheeler
Cover design and photo composite by Trent Truman
Cover art from R&H Photo Library
Interior design by Candy Harvey
Electronic makeup by Shirley M. Bolivar
Typeset: 11/12.5 Bembo

PRINTED IN U.S.A.

10  09  08  07  06          5  4  3  2  1

**R&H Cataloging Service**
Yeagley, Lawrence Robert, 1933-       .
      Beyond anger.

      1. Anger.   I. Title.

          152.4

ISBN 978-0-8280-1943-9

Other books by Larry Yeagley:

*God's Gift of Forgiveness*
*Life After Loss*

**To order, call 1-800-765-6955.**

Visit us at **www.reviewandherald.com** for
information on other Review and Herald® products.

# DEDICATION

*In gratitude I dedicate these pages*
*to the terminally ill patients in hospice care*
*during my 26 years as volunteer chaplain.*
*They faced illness courageously*
*and taught me the value*
*of refusing to hold grudges.*

# Contents

# INTRODUCTION

Randy, a six-foot-three Texan, met me in the lobby of a large hotel. "I've been waiting for you because I want to talk to you before the meeting begins. You see, I'm in charge of this chapter of Victims of Violence. Our program chairperson told me you know a lot about grief, but she didn't tell you one important thing. Mister, we have a lot of anger in this group, and we have a right to be angry. We don't want you trying to take our anger away. As long as you understand that, we'll get along just fine."

Telling him how pleased I was to be invited, I avoided the topic. I didn't dare explain to him that a vital part of my presentation had to do with anger. He was a lot taller than I, and I didn't want to tangle with him in the corridor of the hotel.

As soon as we arrived at the meeting room, Randy began the session. One by one the members of the support group told of tragic deaths, their voices filled with deep anger, and constantly stressed how they wanted to take revenge on the criminals involved. By the time someone introduced me, I could feel the intense emotion in the room. Everyone had full cups of coffee in front of them that they sipped anxiously as I began my lecture.

I told them that anger was a legitimate and natural emotion when a murderer rips a loved one away from us. It is a normal part of grief, but when everything possible has been done to bring justice to bear, clinging to that anger and nursing it can interrupt the healthy flow of healing grief. We can choose to harbor grudges and constantly desire revenge, or we can forgive. Holding tightly to anger will only slam the door to any positive future.

As I spoke I watched the lanky cowboy and his wife as they squirmed in their chairs. They took trip after trip to the coffeepot for a refill, but upon returning to the tables they forgot where they had previously sat. Their faces were flushed. I thought they would tell me to sit down at any minute, but I was determined to deal with my topic. When I finished my lecture the leader abruptly closed the meeting and never thanked me for coming.

My son was seated next to a blond in her early twenties. "Is that your father?" she asked. Steve nodded and listened to her story.

"When my brother was murdered, I was furious," she began. "I wanted to personally end the life of that snake in the grass, but I knew that taking revenge would not satisfy me, even if I killed him again and again. I knew in my heart that I had to forgive him for my own peace of mind. Although I honestly made every effort to do so, my parents' anger has taken on more and more intensity. While I had been victimized by the man who had murdered him, now I was being victimized by the fury of my parents. I couldn't sacrifice my peace of mind, so I moved into my own apartment two weeks ago. The man in charge of the meeting tonight is my father. He and my mother are destroying themselves, but I cannot allow them to destroy me. You tell your father to keep saying what he said tonight. It took a lot of guts to tackle the anger problem in this group, but it needed to be addressed."

I left the hotel knowing that the daughter would face her future with confidence, but that her parents would find themselves imprisoned by their own hatred.

Bonita vowed every day that she would gouge out

the eyes of the drunk driver who took her son's life. During the three months she came to my office she swore that she would grieve bitterly and loudly for the rest of her life. Whenever I tried to tell her how she could move through her grief, she'd always reply, "I don't want to stop grieving. If I lessen my grief it will be disrespectful to my son. If I stop grieving that no-good woman will think I have forgiven her, but I will never forgive her, and I will never stop grieving."

Eventually Bonita's husband moved out and rented a little cottage for him and their surviving son. "I love my wife," he told me, "but I can't put up with her anger. She has driven us out of the house by her refusal to grieve. I told her she would have to forgive the driver for her own good, but I haven't been able to get through to her."

Three years after her son's death, Bonita stopped by my office. Still angry, she wept at the slightest provocation. She was now living alone, a victim of her own refusal to forgive.

A man in his early 30s barged into my office. His eyes flashing, he announced, "I'm going to kill the president. Hear me? I said I'm going to kill the president. I know exactly where he is going to be for the next few weeks." He pounded his fist on my desk hard enough to sprain a wrist. Quickly I slipped from my chair behind my desk to the door. I actually feared for my safety.

Between unrepeatable profanities he told of failed attempts to get a start in life. He said the fat cat politicians never give the little guy a break. The president could put a stop to unfair labor practices so that an uneducated person like himself could get a good job.

His rage increased as he ranted on, and his loud voice carried to my secretary's office. Concerned, she called the hospital security officers. Before they arrived I managed to get his name and address, then invited him to visit me after he had a chance to get some rest and calm down.

Slowly he left the office and walked down the hall, yelling, "You watch the papers, chaplain! I'm going to kill the president! You'll see!"

Returning to my office, I phoned the local office of the Federal Bureau of Investigation to report a possible assassin. An agent took my information and promised to get back to me. Two days later he stopped by the office to thank me for my vigilance. "We did a thorough background check and have determined that he is not a threat. He has developed an anger management problem. While he has received some treatment, he doesn't stay in the program long enough for it to help. Anything that goes wrong prompts more anger. Contacting him, we suggested that he seek counseling again."

Anger is rampant in our modern world. Coaches of professional sports model angry behavior at nearly every game. Pacing up and down the sidelines, they yell, scowl, and swing arms with closed fists. If they disagree with an umpire's call they almost touch noses with the official as the two shout insults at each other.

Movies portray extreme anger as do countless television shows. Children find themselves exposed to toxic talk in the home and even in school at the hands of bullies. The latter has, unfortunately, been true for years. I was in elementary school during the 1940s. Every noon recess crowds of students gathered around as two boys fought until one gave up or received a bloody nose. The encounters never ended with forgiveness, and often resumed another day.

I spent my seventh grade in a one-room school in Peach Bottom, Pennsylvania. The school superintendent decided that eighth graders would be bussed to Robert Fulton Junior High School the following year. It was a frightening experience because we found ourselves caught in an on-going conflict. The big ninth grade boys hated Ben, the African-American student who lived next door to the school. One day they waited at the top of the open stairway. When Ben walked by, they leaped from the stair railing, knocking him to the floor. Immediately six big boys grabbed him and carried him to the water pump at the edge of the campus. One boy pumped vigorously while the rest held Ben's face under the flow of water until he began gasping for air. Somehow Ben managed to free himself and ran home. At the end of recess he returned with his pockets full of stones. When he hurled them at the other boys, they fled inside the schoolroom.

The racial anger and hatred in the hearts of the White students didn't lessen in spite of the teacher's scolding. Ben stayed in school, but he was always apprehensive, expecting another attack. No one made any attempt at reconciliation. I was relieved when my father bought a farm 50 miles north, and I could leave Robert Fulton School.

One day my neighbor children were playing with their dog in their own yard. The dog wandered into the yard next door. The man of the house bounded out the back door of his house. Pointing his shotgun at the children, he yelled, "Get that dog out of my yard or I'll shoot!" I heard his angry voice an eighth of a mile away. Forgiveness? Hardly. The children's parents sold their home and moved to another location.

Years ago I began to suspect that clinging to anger and revenge damages us emotionally and physically. Psychologists and medical researchers have also concluded that out of control anger has an effect on health. While such studies can produce mixed results, most of the evidence gives anger and resentment poor grades.

A growing number of mental health professionals are

11

writing about the need for forgiveness and are teaching people how to do so. Some approaches have a spiritual basis, while others lean heavily upon the power each person has to choose to forgive. Still others see forgiveness as a joint venture between the human and the divine.

Unfortunately, uncontrolled anger has caused some to view all human emotion negatively. I have met abused women and children who have blanked out all emotion. When asked how they feel, they shrug and reply, "I don't know." This is unfortunate because human emotions are gifts from God to make life full and rewarding.

Many picture forgiveness as only for wimps. I've met some parents who tell their children to fight for their rights. But teaching them conflict resolution would be much better. A child should learn that it is a sign of maturity to confront provocation constructively rather than to hold grudges. Forgiveness requires strength.

We can make the transition from anger to forgiveness more easily if we understand both. Unfortunately, articles and books on this topic can be extremely confusing to those unaccustomed to clinical language. Some authors approach this area from a purely secular viewpoint while others incorporate biblical concepts into their writing. A few religious authors, however, totally discount anything written by behavioral scientists. They blind themselves to valuable insights that support and even illuminate biblical principles.

In the following pages I will attempt to glean from both the sciences and Scripture concepts that will help us to live in harmony with one another.

# Chapter 1

# EMOTIONS–GOD'S GIFT

The haunting strains of Ferde Grofés *Grand Canyon Suite* have filled our living room many times during the past 50 years. When I listen to it, I picture the sun rising over the 200-mile long and one-mile deep gorge. I visualize the changing shades of pinks, reds, and browns. The music portrays a desert storm's thunder and lightning. I can almost feel the rain pelt my face as I mentally stand near the rim. The grandeur of the sounds stirs my emotions until I wave my arms, maestro-like, through the last half of the composition. When the music stops, my heart is beating faster, and I long to visit the canyon vicariously again and again.

In the summer of 1990 I physically walked to the rim of the Grand Canyon. As I gazed at its breathtaking enormity in disbelief, a host of emotions instantly washed over me—surprise, awe, joy, humility, and peace. My emotions were so complex and intertwined that I couldn't readily pinpoint individual feelings. I'm still sorting out the full impact of the Grand Canyon on my soul.

My emotions, combined with my view of the phenomenal gash in the Arizona landscape, made my life richer. Apart from my emotions, however, the canyon would have been a mere blip on my memory screen.

Emotions enhance our spiritual well-being. They affect our glands, heart rate, breathing, and perspiration. Beyond that, they bring depth to our character.

The Creator wisely endowed us with the ability to feel. His gift brings us excitement and happiness when we see our newborn. Exhilaration overtakes us when we dive into a cool lake on a hot summer afternoon. Our feelings of hunger seem to vibrate as we behold a table adorned with our favorite dishes. Tears of sorrow spill over our cheeks as we bid farewell to a loved one. Fear floods us when anything threatens us or a friend. Anger stabs us when we see a raging parent slap a child. The desire to stand for justice, decency, and unity is possible because the Creator blessed us with emotions.

I was grateful for emotions when I saw my wife the first time. Wearing a gray skirt and a light-blue sweater, she was leaving the high school library with her books in her arms. I felt an excitement beyond words as I told myself that I *had* to get to know her. Our first social time together left me feeling warm and comfortable with her.

A few years later I stood next to the minister and watched her walking down the church aisle on her father's arm. The minister was sweating in the Washington, D.C., June heat, but I was oblivious to the temperature. Love swept over me, and I couldn't believe our wedding was really happening. I was so happy that God gave me the gift of emotions. Fifty years have elapsed since that day in 1955. My emotions and those of my wife are still a Godsend to us. Without emotions our life together would have no meaning.

Satan is determined to deny us happiness both here and in eternity. He attempts to distort the life-enriching emotions. The emotion of anger seems to be his favorite target. If he can twist and use it for selfish purposes, he can destroy relationships, families, and even nations.

Out of control anger and grudges have torn apart churches. The recent trend of planting new churches has given some an excuse to separate from fellow Christians they cannot tolerate, rather than confronting the issues that divide them. Raging hostility has brought to my office wives with bloody noses and black-and-blue eyes. Because of it I have counseled children who blame themselves for their parents' divorce. The cancer of resentment and rage is eroding the foundation of love, leaving homes in ruins.

God never meant for our emotions to destroy anything. Even anger is not wrong or sinful in itself. No emotion should disturb our spiritual and mental equilibrium. It is what we do with them that can become dangerous. Our emotions can draw us closer to God, but when they become distorted, they can pull us away from Him.

Eugene H. Peterson put it so well when he wrote, "These bodies of ours with their five senses are not impediments to a life of faith; our sensuality is not a barrier to spirituality; it is our only access to it. . . . In company with Jesus, these bodies of ours so magnificently equipped for seeing, hearing, touching, smelling, and tasting, climb the mountain . . . where, in astonished adoration, we are trained to see the light and hear the words that reveal God to us" (*Christ Plays in Ten Thousand Places* [Grand Rapids: Eerdmans, 2005], p. 198).

William Barclay wrote: "There must be anger in the Christian life, but it must be the right kind of anger. There would be something essential missing in a man who had lost the faculty of being angry. Crossness and bad temper and irritability are without defense. But there is an anger without which the world would be a poorer place. The anger which is disciplined into the service of Christ and our fellow man, and which is utterly pure and utterly selfless, is one of the great dynamic forces in the world" (*The Letters to the Galatians and Ephesians* [Philadelphia: Westminster Press, 1958], pp. 184, 185). He then gives the example of the blazing anger of Wilberforce against the slave trade.

Anger is healthy when it alerts us of danger or a threat to our self-respect. It motivated several mothers who had lost a child because of the crime of drunk driving. Their organization, Mothers Against Drunk Driving (MADD), has encouraged stricter laws and harsher punishment for violators. Widespread anger prompted Amber Alert, a program to cut down on child kidnapping and murder. And it has even initiated movements that promote research for the cure of diseases.

"There is an indignation that is justifiable, even in the followers of Christ. When they see that God is dishonored, and His service brought into disrepute, when they see the innocent oppressed, a righteous indignation stirs the soul. Such anger, born of sensitive morals, is not a sin" (Ellen G. White, *The Desire of Ages,* p. 310).

Jesus was a good example Himself. The religious leaders of His day had turned God's gift of the Sabbath into a burden. Instead of being the reminder of God's power to create and restore, it had become a day to dread. And instead of being a reminder that God is in the business of spiritual growth—a time of overflowing joy—leadership had turned it into a day of gloom. They had fixated on what we can or cannot do on the Sabbath rather than on what God meant the day to do for us.

Jesus became angry because the haughty leaders would deny healing to the crippled man who had approached Him on the Sabbath. Christ's anger was not vindictive, but an expression of His great sorrow over their slamming the doors of hope and life closed to innocent people. We find his response in Mark 3:5. "And after looking around at them with anger, grieved at their hardness of heart, he said to the man, Stretch out your hand. And he stretched it out, and his hand was restored."

Although I did not heal a withered hand, my righteous indignation once saved a poor man's income and taught three boys a good lesson. I was driving down a road near Elyria, Ohio, when I saw the boys steal six boxes of strawberries from a makeshift fruit stand in front of a simple home. When they realized that I had seen them, they ran up a driveway across the road.

Turning into the driveway, I cornered them. Their only escape route was to jump a fence next to a briar patch. I leaped over the fence and grabbed one boy by the arm. The berries spilled, and the briars snagged their clothing. They begged for mercy.

"OK, boys, pick up all the berries and then get into my car," I ordered. "You are going to return the berries to the owner." Then I escorted the frightened boys to the man's door where they confessed what they had done. The elderly man was very wise. He invited the boys into the house. "I have a mind to phone the state police and have all three of you arrested, but I have a better plan. This man and I will stand here while each of you calls his father to come pick you up at my house. You can tell your father what you did."

Afterward I learned that the elderly man lived on a small fixed income. He used the strawberries in his backyard patch to supplement his monthly check. Walking back to my car, I felt justified that, because the poor man had been oppressed, the wrong had been made right, and the boys may have been prevented from going down the wrong road in life.

A group of women in a large city near my home also experienced righteous indignation. The drug dealing in their housing complex incensed them. Law-abiding residents faced constant danger of someone robbing and killing them. Some of the residents moved, but most were elderly and too poor to relocate.

The women formed a coalition with the narcotics team of the police department. As a result of the group's vigilance and quick reporting of suspicious activity, the drug dealers left the complex. The women took back their homes because they reacted positively to their anger.

My wife taught in a one-room school after finishing her college training. We visited the parents of her students before school opened. One mother met us in the driveway of her home holding a newborn baby. Urine dripped from the baby's diaper. As she held her poorly clad infant at arm's length she asked, "Would you like to buy a baby?"

When the woman's school-age daughter came to school, my wife noticed many signs of neglect. The girl seldom had a lunch. My wife was angry about the offer to sell a baby. Now the condition of the helpless little girl in her first grade class intensified that feeling. She called the authorities responsible for protecting children from abuse. They investigated and found that the mother had sold the newborn as well as other children in the past for booze money. The authorities removed the little first-grader from the home.

"Was Cynthia upset about leaving home?" my wife asked the social worker.

"She seemed delighted to be leaving home. In fact, she told me she surely hoped she didn't have to eat any more peanut butter sandwiches. That's about all she received at home."

My wife's positive anger behavior saved a little girl from a life of misery. Hopefully, she prevented any more newborns from sharing the fate of their siblings.

I was thankful for the emotion of anger in New Haven, Connecticut. As I entered the church where I was a pastor, my third grade son came running from the schoolroom adjoining the church. As he headed for the basement sobbing, I hurried after him. Then, as I held him in my arms, he described how other students had bullied him for weeks. On this particular day he had drawn a picture in art class. A classmate crumpled it into a ball, threw it on the floor, and stepped on it.

My heart ached for him, and the anger I felt became a powerful protective force. Marching into his classroom, I told his classmates that they had to stop terrorizing my son. If they did not, I threatened to speak to the parents of each student involved. The intimidation ceased, giving me ample opportunity to find another position where school would be less stressful for my son.

The gift of emotions provides us with the heart to reach out to the downtrodden and the disenfranchised. Emotions stir us to engage in causes that promote justice and peace. Without emotions the church would be apathetic and devoid of all compassion. It would become totally inward-focused and without mercy toward others, even those within its walls. Without such emotion the church would sink millions of dollars into real estate rather than ministering to the hungry. And without emotions the church would be a corporation more interested in the latest financial statement than in alleviating human suffering.

Once I attended the open house of a magnificent religious structure in a major metropolitan area a quarter century ago. The guide told us that his denomination erected such buildings all over the world. This new one had cost $82 million. Its spires dominated the skyline for miles.

My emotions shifted into high gear because I had worked for three years in a poverty-ridden and crime-ridden area of the same city. "How can your church leaders justify erecting lavish complexes costing millions of dollars in the light of human hunger and suf-

*Misunderstood Emotion* [New York: Simon & Schuster, 1989], p. 138). Hate, both the consequence and driving force of aggression, "is hardened hostility" (Neil Clark Warren, *Make Anger Your Ally* [Brentwood, Tenn.: Wolgemuth & Hyatt, 1990], p. 90).

The therapist at a large psychiatric hospital pulled old boards from a barrel. Turning to a group of depressed patients, he said, "We have an important project at our hospital. Your help is important. We need to have these boards sanded smooth and free of old paint. Each of you is expected to finish a board within the next five days."

Every day the therapist criticized them for working too slowly or for sanding in the wrong direction. He never encouraged or affirmed them. On the fifth day he carefully scrutinized each board, scolded them for flaws in workmanship, then broke the boards across his knee and threw the pieces into a trash bin.

The therapist told me he was exorcizing their anger. He sought through his extreme provocation to trigger an outburst of rage. It was not my first exposure to this treatment method. My training as a hospital chaplain included a three-hour marathon by a specialist in anger management. He sought to rid me and my classmates of "pent up" anger.

Suspecting what the man would do, I made a pact with a priest friend of mine. We vowed that we would never make eye contact with the presenter. Nor would we speak during the session or respond to him nonverbally. Besides cursing us and accusing us of immorality, he ridiculed our clothing and our hairstyle. After 30 minutes of haranguing, his face became red with rage. Then he stomped out of the room, never to return.

Both of these therapists had adopted the Freudian concept of anger, sometimes referred to as the hydraulic model. A hydraulic jack accumulates pressure with every movement of the pump handle. When the pressure rises sufficiently, the force of the pressure can lift an object many times the weight of the jack.

This once widely accepted theory proposed that every provocation causes anger to build up like the pressure in the hydraulic tube. When the anger reaches a certain level, people are apt to act out, hurting themselves or others. Should the anger turn inward, depression would result. A number of self-help authors who claim that anger focused inward equals depression have adopted this theory.

Building on the concept, many therapists advocated venting anger—letting off steam through yelling, punching, and kicking. They encouraged aggression, whereas many mental health professionals now believe that aggression actually begets aggression.

A young Methodist pastor in chaplaincy training with me once told about her experience in another hospital. The instructor believed that everyone has anger lurking inside that must be removed. He subjected her to primal scream therapy. "Four big guys held me tight against the floor and would not allow me to get up until I had screamed for a length of time they deemed sufficient to rid me of anger," she said. "I screamed, not because I was angry, but because I was afraid of what those big guys would do to me if I didn't."

Archibald D. Hart maintains that if we can store up or accumulate anger, we should also be able to do the same with love, joy, envy, and a host of other emotions. But emotions do not accumulate because they don't exist as single entities. Anger is actually part of a bundle of many feelings.

During my 30 years of conducting bereavement support groups, I discovered that anger is often only one fragment of emotion that receives that particular label. Anger is often intertwined with a conglomerate of other emotions. Grieving people have told me that for them anger is secondary to feelings of disappointment, loss of control, sorrow, and despair. They often tell me they don't know *how* they feel. Being bombarded with a host of emotions makes it difficult to label individual feelings. They say they are confused and overwhelmed. For them, anger is not some "thing" or "entity" that collects in their psyche.

William R. Miller and Kathleen A. Jackson reject the idea that venting is therapeutic. "Nothing in the physiology of anger suggests any kind of cumulative buildup that requires discharge. The catharsis model of therapy for anger is not and never has been supported by sound scientific data. There is no demonstrable therapeutic benefit to be gained from the sheer ventilation of angry feelings or from engaging in aggressive acts, even against imaginary targets such as pillows or empty chairs. This hydraulic theory of anger is simply mistaken in its assumptions about how human beings function" (*Practical Psychology for Pastors* [Englewood Cliffs, N.J.: Prentice Hall, 1985], p. 288).

My wife learned that letting off steam can be hazardous when she was cooking vegetable soup in the pressure cooker. Before the cooker had cooled down she removed the lid. For the next two hours she scraped vegetable soup off the ceiling, the walls, and the appliances. It was not a pretty picture. Neither is it a pretty picture when venting rage shatters marriages and sends victims to emergency rooms and sometimes to morgues. I've see them go to both places.

Diagnosed as suffering from endogenous depression, a friend of mine was admitted to the hospital where I worked. The group therapist learned that Earl didn't get along with his brother-in-law because the latter was constantly finding fault with his workmanship. Mistakenly assuming that Earl was full of anger, he pushed the man to vent his anger on the telephone. "Make sure you cuss him out and tell him to go to the hot place," he told my friend.

I was sitting near the phone in the patient lounge when Earl called Mark. Earl did all the talking. He yelled and profanely told his brother-in-law to go straight to hell. Then he slammed the phone into its cradle. Noticeably shaken, he ran to a chair in the corner of the lounge, lowered his head into his hands, and wept.

Plagued by guilt for behaving rudely, Earl soon became deeply depressed. Such behavior was not typical for him. He questioned whether God could ever forgive him for his unkindness to Mark.

If anger turned inward causes depression, thought the therapist, then anger turned outward would lift the depression. As Earl discovered, it doesn't work

Carol Tavris aptly wrote, "Our contemporary ideas about anger have been fed by the anger industry, psychotherapy, which too often is based on the belief that inside every tranquil soul, a furious one is screaming to get out. . . . Therapists are continually 'uprooting anger' or 'unearthing' *it,* as if it were a turnip" (*Anger: The Misunderstood Emotion,* p. 23).

Beating out the anger was the method a therapist applied to a gentle Christian woman in her late seventies. She had entered the hospital diagnosed with depression. The staff took her to a padded room and gave her a foam rubber bat. The therapist also had a foam bat that he swatted her with. The woman never struck back, but after 15 minutes she fell to the floor in a heap, weeping, "Leave me alone."

Afterward she told me that shortly after her admission to the hospital her husband and her daughter died suddenly and tragically. Bowed down with grief, she had no anger to be beaten out or uprooted. Instead, she was just a kindhearted woman whose world had suddenly shattered.

I went to the treatment team conference to plead her case. The chief of psychiatry ordered the bat room therapy stopped. He asked me to help her to grieve actively for her losses. As she did so her mood lifted and she was discharged.

During the nineteenth and twentieth centuries many theoretical ideas about anger slowly left their mark on Western thought. The belief that we can and must control anger gave way to the belief that we *cannot* and *should not* manage it. The result was that therapists advocated venting.

If venting reduces anger, I have not noticed it in the divorce adjustment groups I have conducted. During the first 90-minute session with 15 divorced women I found myself in the middle of a proverbial hornets' nest. They began expressing their rage at their ex-husbands. The more they did so the angrier they became. Some of them had been divorced for years, but their anger had not diminished because they had been rehearsing their grievances in their minds and with anyone who would listen. They talked obsessively about their experience of betrayal and rejection.

At the beginning of the second session, I became more assertive by making the following speech. "Last week I listened to you rage against your ex-spouses. Your venting didn't lessen your anger—rather it intensified. As long as you rage you cannot concentrate on constructive ways of regaining your equilibrium and living the rest of your lives with purpose and satisfaction. Today I will not tolerate any recounting of injury. We will focus on assessing what you have left and the good qualities that you can celebrate and develop."

The next four weeks we spent evaluating their personal qualities and examining constructive ways to react to the situation of divorce. I emphasized that anger is ideally a temporary reaction to divorce, but that they must not allow it to become a way of life that destroys them, their children, and their other relationships. They discovered that talking about the offense repeatedly can freeze a hostile disposition and have a negative effect on the body. It can prevent a person from learning from the experience. All the women agreed that they did not want to dwell in victim land. Instead, they wanted to spend their energy in self-improvement.

Carol Tavris emphasized that anger does not accumulate. Rather, we continue to feel it afresh because we insist on rehearsing the injury daily, even for months and years. She believes that venting and lashing out intensifies anger and leads to an anger habit. We can get to the place where we explode at the slightest provocation. "When you allow a child to scream, kick, hit, or smash objects, you are not reducing the child's anger. You are increasing his aggressiveness. You are teaching a cathartic habit" (*Anger: The Misunderstood Emotion,* p. 146).

"Most of the time, . . . expressing anger makes people angrier, solidifies an angry attitude, and establishes a hostile habit" (*ibid.,* p. 159).

"Yelling offensive words and honking furiously do not relieve your anger. They make it worse, both by pumping up your own blood pressure and by causing the target of your wrath to yell back at you, which in turn makes you feel angrier yet" (*ibid.,* p. 177).

I enrolled in a class called on human relationships at Gordon-Conwell Theological Seminary. To my surprise, the entire semester consisted of a sensitivity training program. The facilitator claimed to be a Christian minister, but he was belligerent, vulgar, and provocative. He harassed us until some in the group were in tears, and then he left the classroom. Comforting one another, we would discuss our frustration, disappointment, and anger at the facilitator. As weeks passed, our attitudes toward him became negative and bitter. We realized that our hatred of his behavior was rapidly becoming hatred of him. Our venting only increased our anger and resentment.

In spite of many research projects that quash the theory of venting, some therapists continue to base their treatments on it. Even more unfortunate, many lay people give themselves permission to practice venting, thinking that it is healthy. One man told me that getting it off his chest by yelling and pounding his fist on a table makes him feel better, but it only made people close to him feel worse. His behavior was jeopardizing his relationship with his wife and children.

When I fly I never use the earphones for the on-board movie. From time to time I catch a glimpse of the picture and notice that the predominant emotion displayed by the cast is one of out of control anger. And when I visit an arcade to get in touch with youth culture, I notice that negative anger behavior is the norm for video games.

I went to my first and only professional hockey game with our son in Kansas City. Every time someone hit the puck into the net the fans yelled and whistled. Several times, though, I heard cheering even when I didn't see anyone making a goal. "What are they cheering for?" I asked my son.

"Look at the center of the rink. There's a huge fight. People love fights," he said.

Glancing toward it, I saw helmets and hockey sticks flying through the air. Players were slugging each other with bare fists. What a role model for young fans! Is there any question about how young people gain their fascination with violence? Could our culture's misunderstanding about anger be a contributing factor?

Carol Tavris writes that we have no evidence that

competitive sports displace aggressive energy. Instead, high school and college participants are quicker to anger on and off the playing field. They become even more aggressive.

Psychologist H. Norman Wright makes a good point when he says that while the experience of anger is not optional, the way we express it *is*. Every problematic and provocative situation has a positive solution, but out of control anger will not lead to it. It closes off communication, perpetuates irrational thinking, and keeps us feeling like victims.

Newton Hightower relates his experience with helping patients at a Veterans Administration hospital manage their anger. They met every day to yell, scream, and pound pillows. After one week the patients were abusing staff and fellow patients at a greater rate than ever. He begged for two more weeks to see if raging at parents would bring good results, but it did not lessen their rage. The director of the hospital ordered the program to stop (*Anger Busting 101* [Houston: Bayou Publishing, 2002]).

Norman Cousins, while working at UCLA, led an investigation of research projects across the United States that examined the relationship between mind and body. In his book *Head First* (New York: Penguin Books, 1989) he reported on the findings of Dr. Paul Eckman and colleagues at the University of California at San Francisco, School of Medicine. They measured the physiological differences experienced during six emotional states—surprise, disgust, sadness, anger, fear, and happiness. "The results were striking. Not only did significant physiological differences between the negative emotions and the positive emotions turn up, but different emotions produced different effects. For example, anger was characterized by a *high* heart rate and hand temperature increases, whereas fear was accompanied by high heart rate increases and *decreases* in hand temperature. Happiness was associated with *low rises* in heart rate and hand temperature" (p. 134).

Dr. Gary E. Schwartz, of Yale University Department of Psychology, found that anger during exercise raised heart rates an average of 33 beats per minute, more than double the increase during normal exercise (*ibid.,* p. 138).

On February 10, 2005, *The Today Show* featured a report on a new medical finding called *myocardial stunning,* also termed *broken heart syndrome.* At this point researchers have observed it mostly in post-menopausal women. The heart *freezes,* resembling one that would require a transplant to save the patient's life. Timely intervention can reverse the syndrome within days, allowing the person to return to normal activities. The currently known triggers for the condition involve the loss of a loved one, being robbed, a court appearance, and fierce arguing. This is just one more indicator that out of control anger has a deleterious effect on the heart.

You don't have to be a university researcher to learn the physiological effects of anger on the body. Think back to times when you experienced the emotion. You probably remember the sudden increase in your heart rate and the flushed feeling in your face. Sometimes we describe anger as being hot under the collar, which alludes to its noticeable effects on the body.

Part of the cast of a college drama, I played the role of a young man who was upset by the special favors shown to his brother. The brother seldom came home, but when he did, the family pulled out all the stops to make a big celebration. When the brother came to the party, I (his brother) exploded in a rage. I was shocked at how my heart pounded, and I felt shaken to the core. It took me nearly an hour to return to a state of calm. The experience left me weak and lethargic. I was amazed at how much hostility I demonstrated even in a drama.

Another common misunderstanding of anger can be heard on any school playground or in any factory. "That foreman makes me so angry I could spit nails." "Every time I strike out in a softball game, Mack calls me a loser. He makes me so mad." "It's not my fault he has a bloody nose. He makes me mad, and then I slug him." "I can take it just so long, and then I let him have what he's asking for."

Miller and Jackson wrote, "Anger does not follow automatically from situations. Nothing *makes* a person angry. It depends on a certain interpretation in most cases. Just about the only way to keep anger alive is to continue to rehearse injustices mentally. The kind of physical arousal involved in anger is ephemeral. It passes quickly. To be kept alive, anger must be nourished and fed. Anger depends on one's interpretation of the world" (*Practical Psychology for Pastors* [Englewood Cliffs, N.J.: Prentice Hall, 1985], p. 285).

To illustrate their point, Miller and Jackson tell about a couple attending a movie theater. Behind them a child conducted a running commentary on the film. The man became angry and turned to tell the boy to be quiet. There sat a blind man and a little boy describing to his father what was happening on the screen. The boy didn't make the man angry. It resulted from the man's interpretation of what was happening and his choice as to how he would respond to it.

Misunderstandings of anger can prove embarrassing and even tragic. But the Bible can give us insights and the ability to keep relationships peaceful and productive. We will turn to Scripture next.

*Chapter 3*

# ANGER IN THE BIBLE

In an attempt to justify runaway anger some have said, "I don't think it is all that bad. After all, God gets angry. The Bible is full of incidents in which He pours out His wrath. Look at Jesus. He upset tables and swung a whip at the merchants in the Temple. And He said some pretty sharp things to the Pharisees."

Rather than hide behind God's anger to salve our own conscience, it would be better to gain a deeper understanding of divine anger and what the Bible says about human anger.

## GOD'S ANGER

Jesus came to show us the heavenly Father. He openly said that if we see Him, we have observed the Father. He also stated that He and the Father are one. A study of Jesus' reactions to provocation should give us a clearer picture of the Father's anger.

Consider the time when Jesus drove the money-changers from the Temple. In Matthew 21 Jesus turned their tables and chairs upside down. Coins rolled and doves flew. Merchants fled in fear. With a clear voice He told them that they had transformed the Temple into a den of thieves. Was this an act of uncontrolled fury? The answer comes in verses 14 and 15: "And the blind and the lame came to Him in the temple, and He healed them. But when the chief priests and the scribes saw the wonderful things that He had done, and the children who were shouting in the temple, 'Hosanna to the Son of David,' they became indignant."

If I had been in the Temple when this happened, I would never have stayed around if Jesus had sounded vindictive and vengeful. But that was not what He portrayed. That's why the pitiful men and women were willing to sit at His feet right after the clean sweep of the Temple. Archibald D. Hart observed that Jesus' anger totally lacked any selfish involvement. He became angry impartially, always acting in the best interest of the disadvantaged. His anger was not a desire for revenge or a need to hurt in order to relieve His frustration. Rather, He was concerned because the offenders were hurting themselves and the recipients of their short-sightedness.

The greedy leaders loved to see a holiday arrive when worshippers came from long distances. Since it was not feasible to bring a sacrifice from home, such pilgrims depended on buying one at the Temple. The religious leaders required worshippers to buy with Temple currency. The Temple officials slanted the exchange rate in their favor, and the merchants inflated the price of the animals. By the time worshippers purchased the sacrifices, they had little left for the return trip.

The Temple leaders pushed the use of large animals because they sold the meat and the hides to pad their own bank accounts. As a result of the fleecing, many worshippers stayed away from the Temple services and missed the blessings of its worship. Jesus probably noticed the dwindling attendance and was concerned about the people's spiritual well-being.

Eugene H. Peterson stated, "God's wrath is not an

emotional outburst or an irrational fit, but an aspect of his persevering care" (*Five Smooth Stones for Pastoral Work* [Grand Rapids: Eerdmans, 1980], p. 135).

Grace Kellerman and David Hazard observed that "Jesus therapeutically confronted the unbalanced and legalistic spirit of these men" (*When You Can't Say I Forgive You* [Colorado Springs, Colo.: Navpress, 2000], p. 35).

God meant worshipping in the Temple as time to heal the wounds inflicted by the rough places in life. Men and women who felt hopeless could enter and find renewed hope. The troubled in mind could obtain peace. Outcasts could receive acceptance and courage to dream of better days. Worship was to be a time to be still and know God better. But the cold regulations and crooked dealings of the Temple officials and the merchants kept the people away. Jesus' anger came from a heart longing for the children of God to be at one with the Father.

Christ didn't come to our world and die to appease a vindictive God. The entire Godhead devised the plan of salvation out of passionate love for the human family. The cross was not a matter of trying to change the Father's mind. The Father, Son, and Holy Spirit were and are of the same viewpoint. We cannot compare their anger to the explosive and self-centered outbursts of sinners.

In Gethsemane Peter in hot-headed fury whipped out his sword and left the high priest's servant minus an ear, but Jesus rebuked him. "Put your sword back into its place; for all those who take up the sword shall perish by the sword" (Matt. 26:52). From there Jesus went to Golgotha where He cried out, "Father, forgive them; for they do not know what they are doing" (Luke 23:34). His life and death were a far cry from out of control anger. He truly demonstrated anger prompted by heartache for a world in rebellion, a world that He so much wanted to make eternally happy.

Alister E. McGrath said that "the picture of God that is given to us by the cross is that of a deserted, bruised, bleeding and dying God, who lent new meaning and dignity to human suffering by passing through its shadow himself" (*The Mystery of the Cross* [Grand Rapids: Zondervan, 1988], p. 157).

Eugene H. Peterson stated that the death of Jesus is not tragic. It was a carefully defined death, a voluntary fate. He journeyed to Golgotha deliberately and without hesitation. Although His disciples wanted to avoid death, Jesus chose it. It was His substitutionary reaction to the ruination caused by the arch-rebel, Satan. His death was the clearest picture of God's wrath the universe will ever behold. Yet in spite of centuries of study we cannot fully understand it. Throughout eternity we will never cease to be amazed at the cross event.

## ANGER IN THE OLD TESTAMENT

It is interesting to notice how Old Testament people perceived God's anger. The prayer of Ezra during the first Feast of Tabernacles since the days of Joshua is a good example. The returned exiles had rebuilt the crumbled walls of Jerusalem in less than two months. Enthusiasm ran high. Ezra repeatedly confessed their rebellion and declared God's slowness to anger and readiness to forgive. "But our ancestors grew proud and stubborn and refused to obey your commands. They refused to obey; they forgot all you did; they forgot the miracles you had performed. In their pride they chose a leader to take them back to slavery in Egypt. But you are a God who forgives; you are gracious and loving, slow to be angry. Your mercy is great; you did not forsake them" (Neh. 9:16, 17, TEV).

The psalmist sang, "The Lord is compassionate and gracious, slow to anger and abounding in lovingkind-

35

ness" (Ps. 103:8) "The Lord is gracious and merciful; slow to anger and great in lovingkindness. The Lord is good to all" (Ps. 145:8, 9).

Again and again Old Testament followers of God lump His anger with several positive traits such as mercy, love, patience, and goodness. They obviously do not perceive Him to be unfair and ruthless in His dealings with them.

When I became a hospital chaplain, I read all of the book of Psalms, thinking that patients could benefit from meditating on them. It impressed me the number of times the psalmists expressed both their anger at their enemies and their feeling that God had deserted them. Some commentators refer to this as the "absence of God." I also noticed that after a short time of lamenting they would then change the tone of their songs. They ended the psalms by extolling the Lord's goodness and mercy.

Psalm 23 is an example. The psalmist declares that when he walks through deep darkness, God is present to lead him to the light. He mentions that God guides him in round about ways to go in the right direction. God's desire is to have His children dwell forever in His house. The psalmist acknowledges tough times, but God steadily accompanies him through all of them.

During the past 30 years I have worked with grieving people who have suffered tragic and violent losses. I have heard some of them venting anger at God. As they told me their spiritual crises and their doubts about divine fairness their words greatly reminded me of some of the cries in the psalms. This naturally sent me consulting seminary professors and published works on the topic of God's wrath. The explanation that has been most helpful to me is in the *Handbook of Seventh-day Adventist Theology* (Hagerstown, Md.: Review and Herald Publishing Association, 2000). It observes that "God's wrath arises from His holiness and righteousness, and is His response of revulsion toward sin. Since sin is universal, His wrath is also universal. In the biblical portrayal of God's wrath, it appears not so much an emotion or anger as the outcome of deep opposition of His holiness to evil. Divine wrath must not be understood in human terms such as jealousy, vengeance, or vindictiveness. God's wrath is the natural reaction of God's holy love against sin. It is God's moral outrage against human revolt. Without such outrage ultimately manifested in letting His Son die on the cross for the sins of the world, God could not remain God. The most poignant picture of God's wrath against sin is seen in the Lamb of God on the cross. It is God's love that drove Jesus to the cross, and it is His love that manifests itself in wrath against sin" (p. 257).

Perhaps we humans will never fully understand divine wrath this side of eternity. Many, from a sincere desire to feel secure in His love, have sought to explain it. And others will make many more attempts. It is not wise to harshly judge a person who holds a view that is different from our own—after all, there is so much more to learn. I'm not convinced that any of us can describe the nature of God in human language. But I'm sure of one thing: the cross of Calvary is the ultimate argument in favor of God's unconditional love for His creation. All of His other characteristics have to be filtered through His love.

## HUMAN ANGER

The Scriptures eloquently speak about human anger. Mostly they refer to anger that includes aggressive behavior. A few examples follow.

"A gentle answer turns away wrath, but a harsh word stirs up anger" (Prov. 15:1).

"A hot-tempered man stirs up strife, but the slow to anger calms a dispute" (verse 18).

"He who is slow to anger is better than the mighty. And he who rules his spirit, than he who captures a city" (Prov. 16:32).

"Wrath is fierce and anger is a flood" (Prov. 27:4).

"Do not be eager in your heart to be angry, for anger resides in the bosom of fools" (Eccl. 7:9).

I have found these pithy sayings to be very applicable to modern day people. For example, I remember a hot-tempered man who entered a committee meeting uninvited. His loud, blustery voice stunned everyone, and his wild accusations offended and angered the committee members. When he finally departed the room he left the group divided. Some sympathized with the angry man and others disagreed with him. The committee was unable to reach a satisfactory conclusion about the matter at hand because he had stirred up strife.

Once I sat through a heated discussion of some obscure theological topic. People defended their positions with angry voices. Some condemned those who disagreed with them. The anger with which the clergy had lashed out at each other had shocked me. Finally, a wise individual who was slow to anger and slow to speak rose to his feet. In a quiet voice he "captured the city." Smiling, he affirmed everyone for studying the subject and acknowledged their individual views without judging them. He "ruled his spirit" and as a result he calmed the troubled waters. Eventually he was able to convince some of the debaters that antagonistic anger resides in the bosom of fools.

After that experience the words of James had even greater meaning for me: "Everyone must be quick to hear, slow to speak and slow to anger; for the anger of man does not achieve the righteousness of God" (James 1:19, 20).

The apostle Paul established congregations throughout Asia Minor. He had his hands full as contentions arose about doctrines and human relations. Let me share three passages from his writings in which he uses the Greek word *orge,* a term suggesting a settled or abiding condition of the mind, frequently with a view to taking revenge. The word describes long-lasting anger. Paul knew that the church cannot prosper when such anger reigns in the human heart. He strongly condemns such an attitude.

"Let all bitterness and wrath and anger and clamor and slander be put away from you, along with all malice. Be kind to one another, . . . just as God in Christ also has forgiven you" (Eph. 4:31, 32).

"But now you also, put them all aside: anger, wrath, malice, slander, and abusive speech from your mouth" (Col. 3:8).

Paul's admonition to get rid of persistent anger focused on revenge was not only appropriate for his day when the church was in its infancy, but is still relevant even centuries after his time. I met such firmly lodged anger when I was a neophyte pastor.

One day I visited a church member who spent an hour trying to convince me that our congregation should drop another member from membership for stealing from him. When I visited the individual in question, he told me that he had received the items in lieu of salary. Neither man was willing to meet the other to settle the issue. Their anger and resentment had been seething for 20 years. Although they attended the same church, they never spoke to each other. The alleged thief finally moved to another state, leaving the dispute unresolved.

During the past 20 years I have conducted seminars for clergy of many denominations in the United States and Canada. It has saddened me to hear about groups of church members who formed churches of their own as a result of unsettled disputes. The various groups rehearsed their injuries until the offences seemed larger than they actually were. They apparently thought it was easier to separate rather than get beyond the hostility. Mountains replaced the proverbial molehills, keeping people from enjoying God's peace. If Paul could walk into these churches today, he would no doubt say, "Put away all malice so that you can lift up holy hands in worship without wrath and dissension."

People frequently quote the apostle's words in Ephesians 4:26, 27: "Be angry, and yet do not sin; do not let the sun go down on your anger, and do not give the devil an opportunity." Today's English Version renders it, "If you become angry, do not let your anger lead you into sin, and do not stay angry all day. Don't give the devil a chance." Eugene Peterson paraphrased it: "Go ahead and be angry. You do well to be angry—but don't use your anger as fuel for revenge. And don't stay angry. Don't go to bed angry. Don't give the Devil that kind of foothold in your life" (Message).

Ephesians 4:26, 27, rests in the context of Paul's counsel on bringing unity into the community of faith. In verses 23 and 24 he gives us the reason why we can deal constructively with extreme provocation: "Be renewed in the spirit of your mind, and put on the new self, which in the likeness of God has been created in righteousness and holiness of the truth." "Your hearts and minds must be made completely new, and you must put on the new self, which is created in God's likeness and reveals itself in the true life that is upright and holy" (TEV). The Message paraphrase says, "Take on an entirely new way of life—a God-fashioned life, a life renewed from the inside and working itself into your conduct as God accurately reproduces his character in you."

Christians still meet provocations that cause them to "tremble," but by God's grace they can respond in a way that preserves peace and civility. And by God's grace they don't have to rehearse the injury and dwell on the offense.

In the Christian life we will find ourselves provoked and experiencing anger, but when we yield our life to Christ daily, the mind-renewing presence of the Holy Spirit will help us to react in a positive manner. It may not happen overnight. Many Christian writers believe it is a process that will become easier as we continually yield our hearts to God's transforming power.

I saw this happen in Earl's life. His wife studied the Bible with me, and I baptized her on her little girl's birthday. Earl, however, resisted God's voice. One evening he was tired and went to bed early. His 5-year-old daughter stopped by his bedside to say her prayers before she crawled into her own bed. "Dear Jesus," she prayed aloud, "please help my Daddy to love you with all his heart." Hearing it, her father began weeping so hard that the bed shook. That was the turning point in his life. God had spoken powerfully through the voice of a little girl.

Weeks later his wife, Jean, met me at the door. Excited and near tears, she said, "Pastor, I know that Earl has fallen in love with Jesus. I'll tell you how I know. You see, he has been an angry man and used lots of profanity. The least little thing would trigger rage. This week we were making repairs on our rental house. A window crashed down on Earl's fingers. All he said was 'Ouch!'"

The Bible does more than talk about destructive anger expressions. It assures us that we can do all things through Christ who will strengthen us. Earl's transformed life proved that. He and his family had experienced the damage that results from raging anger, but the Spirit's renewing power enabled the family to enjoy love and happiness.

*Chapter 4*

# ANGER IN THE FAMILY

My first job after college was in Pittsburgh, Pennsylvania. We rented the lower floor of a house from Mike and Julia who lived on the second floor. The heating ducts carried their conversations into our apartment, and I imagine they could hear us when we entertained company. I know our sounds carried to the second floor because when my wife was in labor, and we quietly left for the hospital, Julia raised her front window and wished us luck.

Many evenings we listened to them arguing. At first their voices were fairly calm, but in a few minutes the volume escalated to thunderous yelling and name-calling. We would hear heavy footsteps accompanied by swearing, and then the back door would slam shut. Mike would tromp down the long stairway leading from the second floor to the backyard.

The saloon owner was no doubt happy to see angry Mike. After more than enough alcohol, Mike was ready to face the music at home. We could hear him stumble up the stairs and noisily make his way to the bedroom. Julia had a few angry words for him, but Mike was too mellow to respond in kind. In a few minutes all was quiet until the next evening. It seemed to us that the volume and the anger increased as the weeks went by.

By then we had been married only two years. Wondering how two people in love could come to such a sad state of affairs, I hoped and prayed that our home would not become a battlefield. After 40 years in pastoral and hospital ministry I have seen enough Mike and Julia scenarios to convince me that I had good reason to pray for a love-filled home.

The psychiatric hospital where I worked admitted a 15-year-old girl. Long, bloody scratch marks covered her arms and legs. She told me that her mother and older sister went into a rage, pinned her to the floor, and clawed her with their fingernails. Afraid to return home, she requested the social worker to place her in foster care. The only time she ever heard the word "Jesus" was when her mother was angry. The girl asked me if Jesus was a person.

One patient told me that church members highly regarded her father. He would stand up on Sunday morning and do a lot of God talk, but when he returned home he was a devil. She indicated that her father abused her, but did not disclose its nature. Growing up being told that she was a no-good slut, she shut herself off from her father's anger by creating an imaginary world. Unable to believe that she deserved a good husband, she married a man who was just as abusive as her father. That marriage ended soon after the wedding. Constantly in and out of psychiatric treatment, she continues to see a therapist at age 45.

Recently a mother requested that I meet with her 14-year-old daughter. The girl's father had died in a single-engine plane crash a few miles from their house. The mother was sure that his death was the cause of Jeannie's constant anger.

The girl bounced into my office and announced that she didn't have anything to say. I told her that we could at least get acquainted during the hour we'd spend together. She was happy to talk about her "neat" teachers and her "bratty" brother. Before the hour ended, however, she revealed the real reason for her anger.

Her mother began living with her deceased father's best friend three months after her father's death. The two of them spent most of the evening hours in their bedroom with strict orders not to be disturbed. Jeannie perceived that she was losing her mother in addition to her father. In reaction, she refused to clean her room. As punishment, the live-in took off her bedroom door and locked her bicycle in the barn. The two adults kept her room bound for long periods of time. Her mother and her lover spoke harshly to the girl during the little time the three of them were together. Jeannie wished in her thoughts that both of them would die.

At the close of our last session she said, "If my mom would take just a little time to listen to me, I could tell her exactly why I am angry and rebel, but she won't. I have asked her—pleaded with her—but she is too enthralled with the guy who thinks he is now the man of the house."

When I asked her what she saw as the solution to her problem, she replied, "As soon as I'm 18 I'm out of that house. I mean *out* of that house. I can hardly wait for the day."

Jeannie was grieving because of her father's death. Her mother provided no emotional support for her. The anger over her mother's neglect and disrespect compounded the normal anger of grieving. Her anger and the insensitivity of her mother were ripping the family apart at the seams. As I watched Jeannie sullenly go to her mother's car after the last counseling session I was ready to rewrite Colossians 3:21: "Mothers, do not exasperate your daughter, that she may not lose heart."

Family life authors have sought to deal with the

question of why people behave like gentlemen and ladies in the public sector, but feel free to lash out at their family with insults, cursing, and even physical abuse. Some suggest that at home people do not fear any economic consequences, whereas bad anger behavior at work could lead to firing. Others speculate that anger from work gets displaced on family. Several authorities conclude that such people have not learned to communicate, especially about their expectations, feelings, and conflicts. Since every family is unique, there must be many reasons why resentment, rage, and violence occur so frequently in the home.

Mother Teresa said, "Sometimes it is harder for us to smile at those who live with us, the immediate members of our families, than it is to smile at those who are not so close to us" (in José Luis Balado, *Mother Teresa* [Liguori, Mo.: Liguori Publications, 1996], p. 75).

Undoubtedly, Satan is working diligently to unravel the fabric of the home. If he can ruin its environment, he can cause disarray in society. When you read the statistics of the high divorce rate in America, you no doubt get the impression that the devil is having success. And when you realize that divorce is just as prevalent in the church as in the secular world, you have to wonder why the church does not do more to strengthen its homes.

## TOXIC TALK IN THE HOME

A nineteenth-century religious writer, Ellen G. White, frequently addressed the use of angry, toxic words in the home. Consider the following examples.

"Too often the parents are not united in their family government. The father, who is with his children but little, and is ignorant of their peculiarities of disposition and temperament, is harsh and severe. He does not control his temper, but corrects in passion. The child knows this,

45

and instead of being subdued, the punishment fills him with anger" (*The Adventist Home,* pp. 314, 315).

"Unkindness, complaining, and anger shut Jesus from the dwelling" (*ibid.,* p. 422).

"When you are obliged to correct a child, do not raise the voice to a high key. . . . Do not lose your self-control. The parent who, when correcting a child, gives way to anger is more at fault than the child" (*Child Guidance,* p. 246).

"The meekness of Christ, manifested in the home, will make the inmates happy; it provokes no quarrel, gives back no angry answer, but soothes the irritated temper, and diffuses a gentleness that is felt by all within its charmed circle. Wherever cherished, it makes the families of earth a part of the one great family above" (*Sons and Daughters of God,* p. 82).

This author died in 1915, but she felt a need to emphasize the importance of avoiding toxic talk in the home. Apparently, just as now, homes in the church of her day were not practicing the principles of Christian kindness.

James J. Lynch and his research team made some alarming discoveries about the effect of toxic talk on health and longevity. His early findings that resulted in the book *The Broken Heart: Medical Consequences of Loneliness* revealed that premature death rates in Utah were much lower than in neighboring Nevada. He concluded that the high divorce rate in Nevada left people bereft of close relationships. This meant that they lacked sufficient dialogue with others. He referred to dialogue as the elixir of life. Dialogue is sharing all that life is and means to you with others who in turn share with you. His research led him to conclude that the greatest factor in premature deaths from all causes is loneliness.

Medical schools urged him to republish his book, but additional research led to its complete rewriting. In his new volume *A Cry Unheard* he reveals that when we speak we experience a change in vascular rhythm. Exposed to angry, vitriolic speech, the body reacts in terrible distress. When the home constantly has such diatribes, the cardiovascular system becomes exhausted.

This dysfunctional and abusive rhetoric carries into adulthood and then gets passed on to the next generation. "The repetitive and cumulative exposure to language used to hurt, manipulate, control, and offend inexorably led to the serious wounding of self-esteem during childhood. If compounded by other traumatic developmental experiences such as school failure, the effects were both toxic and fatal" (*A Cry Unheard* [Baltimore: Bancroft Press, 2000], p. 4).

"Is it any wonder that parents and teachers alike have great difficulty grasping that when they speak to a child, they literally touch their hearts as well?" (*ibid.,* p. 8).

Lynch's words come to mind when I go grocery shopping and hear parents using caustic, angry, threatening words with their children. My heart goes out to the young people, because I can still recall the burning pain I felt when a church youth leader angrily accused me of being lazy because I wiped the camp tables differently than he did.

One time I saw an 18-year-old French horn player shrink under the harsh criticism of his father. He played his recital piece with fewer flaws than some professionals I have heard performing that composition. But his father was angry because he was trying to build his own reputation by having a brilliant musician son. I wonder how far that young man has gone with his music.

I've had discussions with people who claim that they grew up in homes in which family members let their anger hang out in the open. They blew up and used bad language, but when it was all over they supposedly loved each other just the same. Suzanne K. Steinmetz in her

47

book *The Cycle of Violence* reported on such families. The majority of the examples she studied endorsed the catharsis notion. She found parents who thought it better to spank a child than to restrain their anger. As a result they taught siblings to "fight it out" with toxic words and aggression. Many families regarded screaming matches between husband and wife, or between parent and child, as normal, healthy, and good for relationships.

Carol Tavris, author of *Anger: The Misunderstood Emotion,* found that yelling at each other produces more anger, not less. "Verbal aggression and physical aggression are highly correlated, which means it is a small step from bitter accusations to slaps. . . . Ventilation-by-yelling has no effect on the reduction of anger" (p. 137).

Sad to say, children who grow up in such an environment tend to use toxic talk in their own relationships. Such language has become part of their vocabulary, and they don't consider it inappropriate. According to James J. Lynch, toxic talk can also be a large factor in producing loneliness in a child. That loneliness can easily stay with him or her throughout adulthood.

The apostle James writes that the tongue of the ungodly is full of poison (toxic). While the human tongue is small, it can ignite a mighty blaze just as a little spark can send a forest up in smoke. It burns up our life (see James 3:2-12). Not only does it set the speaker of the words ablaze, it also consumes the spirit of those who are exposed to such toxic language.

Those who live in the fire-ravaged parts of the western United States fully understand such biblical imagery. My wife and I visited Colorado. Driving over a high pass we saw smoke and flames leaping into the sky. An hour later that pass closed to traffic as the flames consumed the forest along the highway. Fires that could not be contained consumed numerous homes and caused the loss of many lives. Angry, toxic words can destroy homes and relationships. We should never be fooled into believing that the free use of them can actually produce a warm and loving family. It is simply false.

The good news is that we can eliminate toxic talk from our homes through divine help. James 3:17 says: "But the wisdom from above is first pure, then peaceable, gentle, reasonable, full of mercy and good fruits, unwavering, without hypocrisy." James even tells us how to acquire this wisdom. "But if any of you lacks wisdom, let him ask of God, who gives to all generously and without reproach, and it will be given to him. But he must ask in faith without any doubting, for the one who doubts is like the surf of the sea, driven and tossed by the wind. For that man ought not to expect that he will receive anything from the Lord, being a double-minded man, unstable in all his ways" (James 1:5-8).

## ANGER AND DOMESTIC ABUSE

A professor of sociology told a gathering of parochial school teachers that domestic abuse is a problem even in the church. She mentioned that pastors too often encourage people to stay in an abusive relationship despite the high risk of injury or even death. Churches and pastors promulgating the unscriptural view of male superiority and dominance may give batterers license to harm their partners and family. Some of the teachers questioned her comment, but I had had too many experiences with abused women to disagree with her.

One woman stopped by my office after her husband had beaten her severely. During the long ordeal she had felt herself fainting, but she kept praying that she would not lose consciousness. She said that she escaped from his clutches only by God's intervention. But when she asked her pastor for help, he told her, "God wants to use you to change your husband. Go home and do everything you can to be a sweet and loving wife." Afterward she left the church office feeling as if the abuse was her fault. Actually taking inventory of all the nice things she had done for him, she planned to increase her acts of kindness. But the abuse continued and became worse.

Another pastor told still another woman that she must have done something to provoke her husband's wrath. Her husband was a church member in good and regular standing. The minister believed that such a good man must have been pushed to the limit. Another clergyman insisted that his female parishioner come for couple's counseling. She told me she refused because she was not an abuser. Suggesting conjoint therapy implied that both parties were at fault.

Domestic abuse is a crime, yet only one in 10,000 acts of battering results in a fine or jail sentence. When punishment does occur, it is rarely severe. Abusers are generally free to return to their homes to repeat their attacks upon people who do not deserve such punishment. People who operate shelters for battered women report that many women return to their abusive husbands when they learn that counseling has begun, but they soon find themselves back in the same dangerous situation.

Emotional, sexual, and physical abuse are all rooted in anger that has turned to rage and criminal behavior. It is important for us to understand this troubling phenomenon. Fortunately, some very excellent studies give us insights into the problem.

Neil Jacobson, Ph.D., and John Gottman, Ph.D., did a 10-year study of 200 couples. They wrote about their discoveries in their book *When Men Batter Women* (New York: Simon and Schuster, 1998). They classified male abusers into two groups: cobras and pit bulls. Cobras actually calm themselves as they verbally abuse their wives.

Violence comes on quickly and the use of lethal weapons is not uncommon. They don't want to be influenced by their wives and have a strong need for immediate gratification. Displaying antisocial criminal traits, they seemingly have no conscience and show no remorse for their violent behavior.

Pit bulls monitor every move their wives make, frequently accusing them of having an affair. Isolating their wives, they expect them to account for all their activities. Often doing a slow burn for 15 minutes or more before attacking, their heart rates and other vital signs elevate during the process of abuse. Exploding into fits of rage, they are less calculated in their violent acts. While capable of chronic and savage brutality toward their wives, unlike Cobras they are seldom violent outside of marriage. After an abusive attack they are often very repentant, attentive, and even romantic, but another slow burn and another abusive episode will eventually follow.

Jacobson and Gottman made some general observations. Once violence manifests itself, they found, it will continue to happen. It may decrease, but it seldom stops. Only 7 percent eventually ceased abusing altogether. When physical abuse lessened, its emotional counterpart increased. Judges who order counseling are giving a mere slap on the wrist. The batterer goes to counseling to get his wife back, and then the abuse resumes. The worst offenders drop out of counseling before it is complete. Prison and counseling together are more effective in holding the batterer accountable.

Professionals dealing with domestic abuse view wives who escape as real heroes. Leaving is dangerous and must be done with the guidance of people trained to counsel victims of abuse. They know how to provide both immediate and future safety. People who do not have the necessary skills should never attempt such guidance.

Groups of professionals pushing for stronger legislation to punish offenders often provide seminars for churches. A pastor is wise to make such education available to the congregation.

## ANGER THAT SPLITS THE FAMILY

Divorce is often the only recourse a person has when abuse seriously threatens the physical safety or the emotional health of the family, but it still has sad consequences. From my pastoral counseling chair I have seen anger and resentment rip marriages and families to shreds. I have heard deep sobbing coming from the depths of the souls of good people who have been rejected and betrayed. And I have watched them plead with an angry spouse to communicate and work toward reconciliation to no avail.

At times I have become bold and confrontational. A couple with three adorable children stopped at my office. The wife was a church member, but her husband was not interested in religion. He awkwardly told me that he did not love his wife anymore and had decided to divorce her. Unable to speak, she wept while he tried to justify his decision.

I firmly believe that if you fall in love and marry, you should marry with commitment. The high-voltage emotion of the honeymoon and early marriage is not a constant. To keep a marriage vibrant and rewarding requires hard work. Marriage is not for lazy people.

These convictions flashed across my mind as I said, "You know what I think? I think you are lazy. Just plain lazy. You believe that marriage is supposed to be a bed of roses, yet you don't spend any time cultivating the garden. I'm not here to tell you how to make a smooth exit from your marriage. I'm here to help you save your marriage. Now, go home, roll up your sleeves, and work on reviving the fire in your relationship." My audacity surprised me.

Two months later I stood on a scaffold painting an 18-foot high ceiling at my church. A young man entered and said, "Preacher, don't bother climbing down. I just stopped to tell you that hard work is paying off. We are happy. It's a keeper."

The hatred and resentment that crippled that marriage vanished because they made a choice to forgive. They decided to open the door to their future instead of dragging the past like a dead weight behind them.

David Augsburger wrote, "It is more prudent to pardon than to resent. The exorbitant cost of anger, the extravagant expense of hatred, and the unreasonable interest we pay on grudges make resentment a questionable pleasure at the least and a costly compulsion at the best, or worst. It is wisest to deal with hatred before the sting swells, before a molehill mushrooms into a mountain, before a spark kindles conflagration" (*The New Freedom of Forgiveness* [Chicago: Moody Press, 2000], p. 19).

Divorce does not end the anger. In many cases the injuries get rehearsed and the stories of abuse and infidelity told to anyone who will listen. Heated exchanges on the phone about visitation and child support payments keep the flames of resentment alive. The anger between ex-spouses filters down to the children. The children become pawns who get moved around from home to home as the battle now centers on those who had nothing to do with marriage's failure. Young people have no choice in the matter. Some of them develop resentment, but nobody seems to care.

Judith Wallerstein studied children of divorce, following them for 25 years. Many were angry at their parents for abuse and neglect. Some took revenge on their parents by using drugs and alcohol, shoplifting, skipping school, and becoming sexually active. Most of the girls she studied grew sexually active by age 12. Boys in their teens became wild and defied their parents' attempt to control them.

Kevin's parents divorced after years of angry and sometimes violent behavior. His father often told the boy that he wouldn't amount to much. After his father moved in with his young lover, Kevin decided to show his father that he really was *somebody*. He began a lawn care business. At first he went from job to job on a lawn tractor. A year later he earned enough money to buy a shiny pickup truck.

Knowing where his father lived, Kevin parked his pickup in front of the duplex and rang the doorbell. Nobody was home, so he jumped over the backyard fence and sat on the deck until his father came home from work. When the father saw his son, he exploded with anger. "What are you doing here? Don't you ever come here without an invitation!"

Kevin leaped over the fence and ran to his truck, then sped away with tears of anger and sadness streaming down his face. "My dad didn't give me a chance to tell him I was successful," he told me. "He didn't see my truck, and I swear he will never see that truck. I will never visit him again." Anger did not die with the divorce.

Rabbi Harold Kushner tells about a resentful woman who sought to hurt her ex-husband 10 years after the divorce. He told her that she was holding a hot coal of revenge to throw at him should he come by, but all the while he was enjoying his new family in another state. All she had to show for her anger was a hole burned in her hand.

Thank God, some people refuse to clutch those hot coals. Marla is an example. After her husband divorced her, she went through the usual grieving process, then decided to forgive him rather than hate him the rest of her life. Five years later her husband was diagnosed with a fast-moving carcinoma. At the time he lived alone in a tiny dilapidated house next to a railroad track in Fort Worth, Texas. The hospice I worked for agreed to care for him at home as long as he could find a primary caregiver. His family had forsaken him so he did not have support from them.

When Marla heard about his situation, she offered to be his primary caregiver. Moving her clothes into a spare bedroom, she tended him until he died. I became acquainted with her when I made hospice visits. She was living proof to me that forgiveness frees a person to forge a new life.

The couple who has a desire to work together can avert divorce. Resentment and rejection send many couples to divorce court, but forgiveness has the power to save marriages. I know because I have seen couples do exactly that.

Kim and Allen were on the verge of divorce when they visited my office. "If you want to learn how to divorce with the least amount of pain," I explained to them, "you came to the wrong place. I'm in the business of saving marriages. Lawyers can describe how to go about divorce in the best way. You need to tell me your intention."

About the same time that Kim discovered that she was pregnant, she also learned that while she was visiting her mother in another state, Allen had spent a night with a work associate. Although extremely angry, she still hoped to save the marriage. Her husband promised her that he would do anything she wanted him to do to make it easier for her to trust him again. When Kim asked him to quit his job and find other work so that he would not have daily contact with his associate, he agreed.

I emphasized that even though Kim was forgiving,

she was not yet fully trusting. He would have to earn her trust. That would require time. On his part it would take patience. They planned to engage in fun activities and restore the early attentions of courtship. Renewing their commitment, they prayed for the daily strength to keep it.

Churches have yet to invest adequately in saving marriages and in preventing anger-terminated unions. Sometimes they put all their eggs in the church growth basket while the marriages in the church are languishing. I know of one congregation that is doing it right.

After conducting a training program for the bereavement support staff at the Richland Hills Church of Christ in Texas, the youth and family life pastor drove me to the airport. As we bounced along in his restored VW station wagon, I asked him, "What do you do that's exciting?"

"I am the volunteer chaplain for the Tarrant County Divorce Court. Couples who are divorcing are required to go through certain counseling classes before divorce is granted. Our church provides the required classes. Frequently a judge orders a couple to meet with me for conjoint therapy. Of course our church members are encouraged to take our classes as a preventive measure."

"Is it working?" I asked.

"It really pays. A number of couples dropped their plans to divorce. Learning how to manage anger and how to communicate, they recommitted to love and cherish."

I knew it was working because of a conversation I had with a young couple seated next to me during the Sunday morning worship service. "Are you members here?" I asked.

"We didn't used to be," the husband replied.

"Our marriage was being torn apart by anger and jealousy," the wife explained. "Counselors told us we should just call it quits. We were headed for divorce. Then we came to the marriage classes at this church."

"Our marriage is healthy now," the husband broke in, "and we are very happy together. We decided that if this church could save our marriage, it could help us grow spiritually."

I congratulated them for their willingness to work at growing their marriage and their relationship with God.

Once I heard a preacher say that families are meant to be little heavens to go to heaven in. While that's rather idealistic, it is still a goal to strive to achieve. My next door neighbors had a fire that gutted their entire upstairs. They lost many of their material belongings. "I learned once again how important family is," the wife commented to me. "I lost things, but we have each other. I am so grateful for family."

## REVENGE OR FAMILY

The Old Testament preserved a story worth visiting. Joseph was his father's pet. In fact, his fancy coat was far superior to anything his brothers ever received. One day the father sent him on a spying mission. Dad wanted to find out if the other sons were doing their job. When Joseph arrived at the brothers' workplace, they became furious. They threw him into a pit and shortly afterward sold him into slavery.

Thanks to God's intervention, Joseph ended up holding a high position in the government of Egypt. His sharp management skills guaranteed that food reserves would be sufficient to see the country through hard times.

Back home his family struggled through a famine. Their father sent the older sons to Egypt to acquire grain, not knowing that they'd be dealing with Joseph. After some testing, he revealed his identity and wept with his brothers. His way of handling the brothers' treachery was inspiring. He told them that they meant to do him harm, but the Lord had instead turned it into something good.

Rabbi Harold Kushner looks at the human side of this story. Joseph named his first son Manasseh, which means "forgetting." Kushner suggests that it indicates that Joseph didn't forget at all. When Joseph sent sacks of grain home with the brothers, he hid his silver cup in one of the sacks. Then he had a scout stop them and search for the cup, the evidence becoming grounds for making them slaves just as they had had him enslaved. It could be that Joseph was tempted to get revenge, but when he saw his brothers' humility and penitent attitude, he could not go through with his scheme. He wanted family more than revenge. No, he did not forget. His brothers' treacherous act was firmly embedded in his memory, but he rewrote his memory of that dark day.

## ANGER AND BALANCE

A minister's wife was having problems with anger, resentment, and depression. She talked rapidly and at times with tears. "I am fit to be tied. I have no life of my own. All I do is taxi my kids from place to place. They have after-school activities every day, and I am the one who is expected to get them to their activities on time. And I'm the one who has to take phone calls from irritating church members. I do the housecleaning, make the meals, do the laundry, and settle arguments. My husband tells me I have to be involved in all the activities at church because it wouldn't look right for the minister's wife to do otherwise. For years I have wanted to take nursing at the community college, but I don't have time to think, let alone go to school. I'm angry at the kids and angry at the church and angry at my husband. I am just mad, mad, mad!"

When I could get a word in, I made some suggestions that she enthusiastically put into operation. "Limit the kids to one extracurricular activity per week," I said, "and tell your husband that you will take one to his appointment, and he can take the other. Order a second phone line for personal and family matters and install an answering machine on the number used by church members. Your husband is the minister. Let him return the calls recorded on the answering machine. Involve yourself with only one activity at church. Delegate the household chores evenly among family members, including your husband. Finally, enroll in one class at the community college."

When she returned for her next appointment, she was more relaxed, was under almost no stress, and reported that her resentment and depression had vanished.

I have observed that disorderly homes, hectic meal schedules, overwork by one or more family members, poor diet, little time for leisure togetherness, many hours of TV viewing, and loud music breed sour dispositions and negative anger behavior. A family out of balance is similar to tires on a car that are not balanced. The car shakes and is difficult to steer. Families out of balance are difficult to manage. The trip is not pleasant.

Standing in line at a Greyhound bus station in Fort Worth, Texas, I watched an elderly man in line ahead of me. He had a worn-out suitcase, its contents bulging through holes and cracks. When he bought his ticket, the agent said, "You planning to put that grip in the luggage compartment?" The old man nodded. "Won't make it, sir," the agent continued. "Let me see that thing."

The agent placed the bulging suitcase on a table and wrapped every square inch of it with silver duct tape. "How's that?" he asked. The old man smiled and ambled to the waiting bus.

Families can become like overstuffed suitcases. Everything jammed into the weekly schedule leaves no room for God. Confusion and extreme stress pushes family members to the limit. Tension and crowded schedules lead to anger and toxic words. Such families need a major overhaul. Balance is essential.

Years ago I saw a *Saturday Evening Post* front cover that spoke eloquently of the affect of anger on a family. It consisted of a series of successive scenes. An angry boss shouts at an employee. The employee goes home and scolds his wife for not having dinner ready. The wife yells at the boy for dragging mud onto the kitchen floor. The boy kicks the dog. The dog chases the family cat. The cat catches a mouse.

Each of us lives in a series of spaces during the week. We have a workspace, a home space, a community space, a church space, and many other spaces. If one of our spaces gets too jam-packed and unrewarding, that space can provoke anger. If not confronted and dealt with constructively, that anger can bleed into the other spaces.

Poorly managed anger filters through the family and into the larger community. On the other hand, an understanding and forgiving spirit permeates the family and makes the larger community pleasant. Henri J. M. Nouwen expressed it well.

"Whenever we forgive instead of letting fly at one another, bless instead of cursing one another, tend one another's wounds instead of rubbing salt into them, hearten instead of discouraging one another, give hope instead of driving one another to despair, hug instead of harassing one another, welcome instead of cold-shouldering one another, thank instead of criticizing one another, praise instead of maligning one another . . . in short, whenever we opt for and not against one another, we make [God's] unconditional love visible. . . . We are diminishing . . . violence and giving birth to a new kingdom" (*Letters to Marc About Jesus* [San Francisco: Harper and Row, 1988], pp. 60, 61).

*Chapter 5*

# CHOICE AND CONTROL

nger is a normal physical preparation for action. It comes when we find ourselves in danger, when someone attacks our values, and when we or others experience abuse. In many ways anger is like the warning lights on the dashboard of my car. They come on when my fuel or battery gets low and when the engine malfunctions. I appreciate the lights, but they are only helpful if I make the right choices in response to their flashing.

If I ignore the lights, I will pay a huge repair bill to rectify a problem that I could have prevented by an immediate trip to the dealership or another garage. Nobody else is responsible for my negligence. I am. It is my decision alone to pay no attention to them. When I feel anger, I am responsible to make the choices that will care for the situation in a constructive manner. I can't blame anyone else for the way I let myself feel and respond.

Years ago I taught grade school. Playground supervision was always a lesson in human relations. Two fifth-graders would get into a tussle. Fists would fly, and sometimes a nosebleed would result. When I broke up the fight I'd hear, "It's not my fault. He made me so mad. That's why I slugged him."

After the excitement died down, I tried to teach the boys that anger is inevitable, but aggression is not a necessary or automatic response. It is something we alone choose. Anger alerts us to a situation that needs our attention and challenges us to correct it in a civil manner. We discussed approaches that they could have used other than a fistfight.

Carol Tavris said that we constantly make choices about how we are going to behave, what we are going to say, and when we are going to speak. "Judgment and choice distinguish human beings from other species; judgment and choice are the hallmarks of human anger" (*Anger: The Misunderstood Emotion,* p. 38).

"Grammatically, the negative, our capacity to say 'no,' is one of the most impressive features of our language. The negative is our access to freedom. Only humans can say 'no.' Animals do what instinct dictates or what training embeds in them. 'No' is a freedom word. I don't have to do what either my glands or my culture tells me to do. The judicious, well-placed 'no' frees us from careening down many a blind alley, from bushwhacking through many a rough detour, frees us from debilitating distractions and seductive sacrilege. The art of saying 'no' sets us free to follow Jesus" (Eugene H. Peterson, *Christ Plays in Ten Thousand Places* [Grand Rapids: Eerdmans, 2005], p. 196).

Andrew D. Lester insists on the reality of human choice. "We must challenge the idea that emotions have a life of their own, separated from our cognitive processes and free to take over our actions without our endorsement. Humans have the ability to control emotions and to use them either creatively or destructively" (*The Angry Christian* [Louisville: Westminster John Knox Press, 2003], p. 63).

Lester again insists that "we have much control over what we perceive as threatening and, therefore, what triggers our experience of anger. Our theologically valid choice about managing anger has to do with taking responsibility for what triggers our anger as well as for the behaviors by which we express our anger. Because an anger event always begins with an interpretation of a life situation, we have responsibility for having created the interpretations that leave us threatened" (*ibid.,* p. 89).

Some years ago I interpreted a certain announcement by my school board chairman as an act of betrayal and hostility toward me. The board asked me to comply with its wishes even though the superintendent of education supported the way I was managing the school. Years later I learned that a prominent board member wanted my job. He persuaded a majority of the board members to approve his motion. The chairman was helpless to change the action. Mentally replaying again and again the chairman's announcement in my mind, I kept anger alive for years. But my interpretation was incorrect. When I met the chairman in another setting and he expressed affection for me and appreciation for what I did in that school, I had to acknowledge my misinterpretation. Changing my understanding of that event was a freeing experience.

I am convinced that the human mind has great power. Terminally ill people have taught me this during my many years in hospice ministry. Some patients clung to life for weeks and months until they have had the chance to meet with all their family members. After accomplishing their goal, they died. A few were in the midst of writing a book. They lived much longer than any medical personnel thought they would. Once the patients finished their books, they died. One man wanted to fulfill a boyhood dream of taking an exotic trip on a large motorcycle. He died shortly after returning. The will to live is powerful.

In hospital oncology units I have seen people go

through aggressive treatment with very little discomfort, because they told themselves the medicine would not make them deathly sick. Others believed the horror stories told them by friends, and they suffered much nausea and other problems.

The same mental ability works in choosing anger response and controlling anger behavior. A man who had been ruining relationships both at home and on the job asked me to help him with his hair-trigger anger responses. The first thing I asked him to do was to keep a diary of his anger episodes. This helped him to understand his anger and learn what types of situations triggered it. Once he identified the major areas of provocation, we worked on ways of reacting. He actually wrote out the wording of his responses and read them aloud to himself. We did all this when he was not upset about anything. I asked him to think about these responses during the day when he was not under pressure. Finally, he prayed and asked God to help him implement his strategies. In the process he learned that God gave him a mind capable of choosing and controlling.

A cardiologist, a pulmonary specialist, and I assisted 3,000 individuals to quit the smoking habit in a large New England city. The experience taught me something important about choice and control. The originators of the cessation plan suggested that we ask those enrolled to repeat hundreds of times a day, *"I choose not to smoke."* But we decided that such a mantra was inherently negative. The word "not" had to go. Instead we asked them to repeat things such as *"I choose to live life to the fullest," "I choose to play football with my children," "I choose to run a marathon next spring,"* or *"I Choose to Reach 100."*

The participants discovered that making positive statements programmed their minds to go in the right direction. The firmer their decision and the more frequently they verbally expressed their intent, the more successful their habit change. Some of them used the same positive use of their mental power to change sedentary and eating habits and to stop swearing.

We need to be careful that we do not adopt a purely power of positive thinking approach to how we will respond to provocation. Rather, we need always to remember that the One who created the mind is at work in each of us, enabling us to control our emotions. The apostle Paul wrote, "Do not be conformed to this world, but be transformed by the renewing of your mind, so that you may prove what the will of God is, that which is good and acceptable and perfect" (Romans 12:2). The more completely we trust God for power to choose the best response to provocation, the more appropriately we will be able to meet it.

We must never leave God out of the equation. A man who successfully stopped smoking reminded me of this. "Larry, you gave us some very sound psychological principles to use, but when you told us about the spiritual dimension of smoking cessation you soft pedaled it. When I used the psychological principles without divine help I could never have quit. You need to emphasize the spiritual more."

God gives us the power to decide how we will handle anger, but He stands by with all the strength we need to go in the right direction. That's why the apostle counseled us to avoid paying back evil for evil. He told us not to take our own revenge, because God will deal with those who provoke us. "If possible, so far as it depends on you," he urged us, "be at peace with all men" (verse 18). God's biddings are His enablings.

When someone claims that we cannot control anger and should not even try, I tell them to read Archbishop Desmond Tutu's book *No Future Without Forgiveness*

(New York: Doubleday, 1999). The Truth and Reconciliation Commission in South Africa heard testimonies of people who had been victims of horrible crimes. Archbishop Tutu wrote, "As I listened to the stories of victims I marveled at their magnanimity, that after so much suffering, instead of lusting for revenge, they had this extraordinary willingness to forgive" (p. 86). They chose to go beyond anger to forgiveness.

During my three decades of conducting bereavement support groups I have met people who have chosen to forgive in situations that amazed me. Parents who lost a son when a drugged driver crossed the centerline of the road went to the jail and told the irresponsible driver that they forgave him. A mother faced the man who beat her son to death. She explained that she had suffered enough from the death of her son and did not wish to prolong the pain by clinging to anger and rage—therefore she gave him the gift of forgiveness.

Corrie ten Boom was a world ambassador of forgiveness. After suffering inhumane treatment in Nazi prison camps and witnessing the deaths of hundreds of people, she returned to Germany to preach about forgiveness. There she met some of the people who had been involved in the atrocities. Naturally, anger welled up in her, but she prayed for God's strength—and then forgave them.

When Jesus entered our mixed-up world, He came because He chose to forgive. His three-year ministry demonstrated His decision to cast our sins into the depths of the sea. He stood before His accusers and persecutors in silent sadness. Hanging on the cross, He declared, *"Father, forgive them; for they do not know what they are doing"* (Luke 23:34). What an example for us!

*Chapter 7*

# HANDLING ANGER

Two elderly sisters living along the Ohio River had become too feeble to haul the wood and coal they used for heating into the house. Every week I stopped by their house and replenished their fuel supply. Their cupboards needed cleaning, but they were too high for the women to reach. "If you clean the cupboards for us," they offered one day, "you can keep any books you find up there."

Finding a stepladder, I was soon hard at work. Before long I pulled out an old biography of Dwight L. Moody. Taking it home, I found in it a delightful story about handling provocation and anger. The renowned evangelist preached at a clergy conference. When he finished, a minister criticized his sermon. In front of the entire group he accused him of stringing a number of newspaper articles together with a few of his own comments added. Moody, he declared, had done a poor job of homiletics. Rising to face his accuser, he quietly thanked the minister for his critique and asked him to pray that next time he could be more effective. His response echoed Matthew 5:25 in which Jesus counseled us to agree with our adversary. One translation says we should quickly make friends with our opponent.

A few months before I read that story, a man spoke up loudly during a sermon I was presenting in church. "I disagree," he said. "That's not what that text is saying." My face turned red, and I could feel the emotion of anger. Unlike Dwight Moody, my reaction was testy and defensive. I was sure that I needed to learn more about how to handle provocation and anger.

For example, I could have said, "Thank you for bringing this to my attention. I certainly don't want to mislead anyone. May I speak with you after the worship service to learn your interpretation? I'll make this text a matter for study and prayer during the week. Then I'll share the results with the congregation next Sabbath."

Since then I have been searching for constructive ways to handle anger. As you read the following suggestions you will probably think of additional ideas. I must mention that there is no quick fix for handling anger problems. The anger habit is usually gradual in the making, so no magic wand will instantly make it disappear.

While the approaches that I give will definitely help, the root of anger problems rests in spiritual issues. For that reason I have taken time to focus on the process of developing an abiding relationship with Jesus. This requires taking the Gospel seriously and applying it to every aspect of life. God holds the power we need to handle anger. Every day we must let that power fill us. This is not a quick fix, but an ongoing and lasting solution.

***Sense your value as a friend of God.*** God accepts you as you are, then makes you more than you are. If you understand that you are precious in God's sight, you can rejoice in your value. Confidence in who you are enables you to face provocation without self-doubt. While God's affirmation of our value is most important, it also helps to associate with positive and affirming friends.

Sometimes provocation can become a frontal attack

on our self-image, resulting in anger. A way to defend yourself against such onslaughts is to strengthen your assurance that you are precious in God's sight even though you have weaknesses.

*Have a realistic worldview.* We cannot expect immunity to threats, hurts, mistreatment, and disrespect no matter how devout we are. Scripture does not promise God's followers that they will always receive fair treatment. Jesus certainly didn't. He mentioned that if He had to endure unfair treatment, then we can expect the same. One author mentioned that a charging bull will not avoid attacking you just because you are a vegetarian. Our worldview must recognize anger as a common human emotion. We must also see it as something that we can meet constructively.

The writer of Psalm 23 teaches us that God's followers will walk through deep darkness, but that He will accompany us on the journey. The path may be winding, but God will guide us to our heavenly destination. The One who also felt hurt, mistreatment, and disrespect will stand by us when we experience the same.

*Understand that you are just as capable of offending as is your offender.* A superior attitude seldom makes allowances for the weakness of others. If you remember the times when you were unkind and insensitive, you won't be as hard on those who provoke you. You'll be able to look at him or her through the eyes of possibility.

*See all people as God's children.* The Bible says that Christ died for us while we were still rebels. By God's grace we can view our offenders as belonging to God.

When I was the pastor of a large city church during the hippie era, some church members became upset because hippies were spending time in the wooded area behind the church. I told them to go out and invite them to worship and to fellowship dinner. Yes, their behavior was sometimes offensive, but God didn't love them any less because of it. The church members were able to forgive them for scattering beer cans on the lawn once they began viewing them as God's precious children.

***Don't rent too much space in your mind to anger.*** Don't give anger a lifelong lease. How do you rent space to anger? By constantly thinking about the offense that triggers it. The more space you allow anger to occupy in your mind, the less room you have available for positive events. The Bible admonishes us to not let the sun go down on our anger. That's the way you cut down on the rental space.

The owner of an Arkansas storage complex had a huge auction. Many renters spent a lot of money storing hundreds of items that they thought to be important. As months and even years passed, the owners no longer regarded the contents of the storage units as that valuable. Rather than get rid of them, they refused to pay the rent. After three months in arrears, the storage company auctioned the items to recoup their lost rent money.

We need to decide whether storing provocations will benefit us. What seems earthshaking today may be of little consequence months from now. Remember, the more space you rent to anger and the longer you store it, the higher the cost to you emotionally, physically, and spiritually.

***Confront anger.*** The emotion of anger signals you that something needs attention. Denying the existence of anger prolongs it and prevents resolution. But confronting anger does not mean that you aggressively attack the provocation. It does demand that you be truthful about what you feel without attacking the offender.

A young seminary student visited his family several times a year. His siblings were not religious and had always criticized his faith community. During one visit two of his siblings stated that he was foolish for falling for religion that was only interested in people's money. They accused church leaders of being hypocritical.

Anger signaled him that he needed to defend himself and his faith. But instead of allowing himself to explode, he calmly told them, "I'm having difficulty understanding something. I have been a member of my church all my life so far. I know its history and am also acquainted with current church practices. You have never been a member of my church, yet you seem to know what's wrong with it. I will accept your evaluation when you become members and know its inner workings. Until then, I must reject it." His confrontation stopped the criticism. Eventually one of those siblings attended the church and had a rewarding experience.

*Plan your responses.* Suppose the same provocation occurs a number of times and each time your anger behavior is negative. When you are calm and not experiencing the stress, spend some quiet time reflecting on various positive responses. You will really profit from such an exercise if you practice them aloud. Repeat the responses until they become natural and automatic.

You might find it helpful to teach yourself how to disagree politely with people during everyday conversation. Learn to do so without offending or seeming opinionated. Also find something in the conversation that you can agree with and can affirm. It is good preparation to meet provocation graciously.

*Avoid irrational thinking.* If you find yourself in a group situation that causes anger, you might assume that people in the group are upset with you and don't want you to be a part of the group anymore. But that may not be the case at all, because it is actually your negative self-talk increasing your anger. A danger is that you may even leave the group abruptly and never return.

By challenging your perception of what is happening

in the group, you may discover that your understanding of the event is wrong. Maybe the person or persons had no intention of offending you.

People going through a divorce may be very angry at the spouse initiating the divorce. Their feelings may be saying, "I am a total failure as a wife (or husband). I must be really ugly and incapable of keeping a mate. I'll never be able to love anyone again." But if they examine their irrational thinking, they may find that such thoughts are not true at all. Meet anger with positive and complimentary thoughts about your value as a person and stretch your ability to see beyond the present.

***Take time before you respond.*** Some would call it *counting to 10 or 20.* Reacting immediately is what we can proverbially call *speaking before putting the mind in gear.* If you have practiced responses while you were calm, taking time can help you use them in the face of the provocation. Sometimes silence is the best way to deal with difficult situations. Several authors I have read suggest that you might say, "Right now I need time to think before I do anything. I'd like to sit down with you tomorrow at your convenience. Yes, right now I am feeling angry, but we can get through this together."

A partner in an engineering firm, Gregory implicitly trusted Anton to handle the financial end of the business, but Anton embezzled thousands of dollars, eventually forcing the company into bankruptcy. First, Gregory took a weekend to contemplate his response after discovering his partner's dishonesty. Then the two of them had a long discussion.

Gregory told Anton that he had forgiven him and wanted to promise creditors that they would be paid in time, but the partner refused to honor the debts. So Gregory visited all those to whom money was owed and promised them in writing that he would personally repay them. By working several jobs and living with only the basic necessities, he cared for the outstanding debts. Forgiveness had a price tag, but he carefully weighed all his options before responding to the injustice. He felt that he had taken the honorable road.

*Have empathy.* A church member grasped a young minister by the lapels and said, "I want you to know that I hate you." Taken by surprise, the pastor soon became angry. He wanted to believe that his parishioners appreciated his work. He felt angry because his dream of being a highly respected pastor seemed to be vanishing.

After a few weeks of careful thinking about the man's situation, however, the pastor saw that the one who hated him was acting out of a personal situation that had left him feeling out of control. The young minister had innocently acted in a way that added to the man's sense of helplessness. When the minister tried to put himself in the member's situation, he was able to see the facts behind the other man's hatred.

*Change your perspective.* It is not necessarily the provocation that prompts anger, but how we interpret the situation and what it means to us. If we view the incident as a challenge to grow personally or to mend a relationship, anger may not mushroom into resentment.

Once I lost a job because of corporate downsizing and felt anger resulting from a loss of security. Fortunate enough to find another position in another state, I had the chance to interview many employees at the new place. During the few days I spent looking over the new position I began to see some opportunities to grow professionally that had not been present in the former job. My perspective changed. The loss of the job eventually led to greater service to the community. The change in perspective actually created anticipation as I began the new position.

*Learn assertiveness skills.* Assertiveness is not aggressiveness. Rather it is protecting your self-respect without demeaning the offender. And it is a necessary quality and skill needed in confronting anger.

A secretary in an organization was angry because the company did not keep its promise of a promotion. The expectations of her supervisor became more and more unrealistic. He even added to her workload jobs from another department. During my one-hour visit with her I taught her how to be assertive on the job.

An hour before closing time her supervisor walked up to her desk with 15 letters to mail. Smiling at him, she said, "Mr. James, I'd be happy to work on the letters in your hand, but you will have to make a decision. Do you want me to finish the work you gave me this morning, or do you want me to drop that and do the letters you have now?"

Rather than being frustrated and angry, she felt she was in control. The supervisor said to complete those from the morning, and then he told her to keep the new letters for the next day. Instead of fuming with anger on her way home, she enjoyed the scenery and the music on her car radio.

*Journal provocations and responses.* Managing anger is not possible if you don't know what triggers it in you. In addition, it is essential to recall and record your responses. Once you have monitored these two items for a few weeks or months, you will know what you need to address.

Early in my ministry I became angry at what I perceived to be disrespect for the standards of modesty among some church members. I found a way of inserting comments about the trend into sermons. What I did not notice was an angry sound in my voice as I presented the sermons. One Sabbath as I greeted people at the end of the worship service, a man shook my hand firmly and asked, "Pastor, who are you angry at?" That burned. I went home and began to look at the sermons I had preached. Then I prayed that I could think critically about the tone of voice that had prompted the member's question. Finally, I concluded that the man was accurate in his assessment. I was angry about something over which I had no control. I knew that my call to the ministry was to speak to the heart while God's work was to transform lives. My careful examination led me to pray before each sermon preparation, "Lord, help me to speak with love and kindness. Give me words to lift up the discouraged and strengthen the weak."

Journaling is similar to a physician who runs tests and listens to the patient's symptoms. After looking at all the test results and a hands-on examination, the medical doctor makes a diagnosis and decides on the treatment. When an angry person understands all the factors of what provoked him or her and evaluates the responses, he or she will then know what needs to change.

***Change your storytelling.*** Anger remains alive and fresh by telling and retelling the story of the wrongs suffered. The story is negative and bitter. Handling anger necessitates transforming the story from negative to positive.

John Coblentz in his book *Putting Off Anger* (Harrisonburg, Va.: Christian Light Publications, 1999) compares an angry, bitter person to an old man carrying a sack on his back. He is doubled over with the weight of all the wrongs and hurts stored in the bag. At every opportunity he tells about the ways that someone wronged him. When a listener expresses sympathy, he says, "Oh, you haven't heard the half of it." Then he pulls more wrongs out of the bag. If the listener doesn't want to listen anymore, the man puts the sack on his back and searches for another person with whom he can share its contents.

Telling the negative story repeatedly develops an anger habit. Deciding to stop rehashing it is a bold step in handling anger in a healthy manner.

Church members often requested me to visit loved ones in prison. Occasionally I had to wait an hour of more to see the prisoner. Some of them spent their allotted time telling me the same tale of injustice and anger. Before long I felt that I could recite the story myself, and I noticed that their anger intensified from one visit to the next.

But I looked forward to my appointments with a prisoner who had forgiven those whom he felt had treated him unfairly. He spent each session telling me about his self-improvement projects and requested resources to prepare himself for a profession. No doubt he initially did his share of negative storytelling, but he changed his story.

Once I read about a civilian prisoner of war who could have allowed anger to consume him. Instead he mastered biblical languages. When the war ended he taught biblical languages in a seminary.

***Pray for wisdom to respond properly.*** The Bible says that we can do all things through Christ who strengthens us. That is a powerful promise to us when we are learning to handle anger. Relying on our own wisdom and techniques is not sufficient. We need to ask God for His aid.

When I was a boy I enjoyed helping my father load sacks of grain onto the farm wagon. As we harvested the wheat field, we dropped the full sacks at one end of the field to be taken to the barn later. I always grabbed the end of the sack tied shut. It gave me something to hold on to. My father, a strong broad-shouldered man, gripped the sack near the middle so that he would be bearing most of the weight. Of course, I went to supper bragging about how I lifted the sacks. My father smiled at my childhood boasting, knowing full well that he did most of the work.

Handling anger is somewhat like handling those grain sacks. We can make noble attempts, but God wants to bear the heaviest part of the load. Together, we can get the job done.

**Look toward the future rather than focusing on the pain of the past.** A certain book written by a pastoral counselor disturbed me. The author operates a counseling center in which he pushes people to dig into their childhood. Urging them to recall all the hurt and pain of growing up, he tells them to experience the same emotions they had when the incidents occurred. Supposedly they will then realize that their present behavior results from events in the past.

Can you imagine driving a car from Los Angeles to Denver while looking only into your rearview mirror? I would not want to be a passenger in that vehicle. Focusing on the past is resurrecting what you cannot change. But you do have some input into today and into your plans for the future. Staring into the past keeps you from enjoying the present.

During a visit to Dorr County, Wisconsin, my wife and I took a boat ride to Washington Island. I saw a woman standing at the back of the boat gazing at the wake. She stood there during the entire trip. I climbed to the top deck and took in the sights ahead. I was able to experience the anticipation of seeing Washington Island up close.

Gazing at the wake of past hurts wastes energy needed for building today and tomorrow. Looking forward to where you might be is much more rewarding than brooding over where you have been.

For seven years I was the chaplain in a psychiatric facility in which a group therapist pushed patients to recall the painful experiences of the past. Once they identified the episodes of pain and again felt the anger, he asked the patients to confront their offenders.

Linda and her college roommate had visited each other through the years and had spent many happy times together. After weeks of group therapy, however, Linda went to the woman and angrily accused her of tiny offenses that had been resolved shortly after they happened. The charges overwhelmed her friend and left her almost speechless. Since then all contact has ceased between them. A beautiful friendship lay in ruins, all because Linda looked in the rearview mirror instead of building on the present.

Pinning the blame for our anger on parents and friends is irresponsible. Nursing anger over things long gone is a massive waste of time. God has given us the power to choose to move beyond the past.

**Accept God's unconditional love instead of trying to earn it.** What does this have to do with handling anger? When we find ourselves amazed at His willingness to accept us, warts and all, we will want to free our offenders to share that same amazement as well.

William R. Miller and Kathleen A. Jackson wrote a pastoral counseling textbook, *Practical Psychology for Pastors*. They devised an approach for examining and managing various problems that employed the acronym STORC. Let's apply it to the management of anger.

*S*–Situations can contribute to feelings of irritability, impatience, resentment, or other forms of anger. Some of them consist of environmental irritants such as noise, inclement weather, physical pain, and too little sleep. We can add frustration and overcrowding to the list.

*T*–Thought patterns can lead to unrealistic expectations that can build us up for a major letdown. Thinking that an event is a threat to our security can cause anger. We need to check our evaluation of events.

*O*–Organic factors influence emotion. The autonomic nervous system gets elevated or aroused, increas-

ing the chances of experiencing anger or aggressively acting on such feelings. Certain stimulant drugs increase
arousal, caffeine, nicotine, and alcohol being some of the
most common.

**R**–Responses to provocation can either make or
break relationships. It is important to review your reactions with a friend and ask them to help you prepare to
respond constructively.

**C**–Consequences of negative responses may gain
what you wanted initially, but you need to analyze the
long-range implications. You may get your own way by
shouting and hitting, but that behavior can mean your
loved ones will leave and you'll be alone and miserable.
*Anger management may require the assistance of a counselor
who can help you make alterations in these five factors.*

Is handling anger in a healthy manner worth the effort?
Indeed, it is. It opens doors for you to grow emotionally
and spiritually. You actually become a partner with God in
making our world more peaceful. And you become God's
resource for drawing others to His eternal kingdom.

# Chapter 8

# FORGIVENESS–THE KEY

Psychology, philosophy, physiology, and the neuro-sciences have sought to arrive at an understanding of anger and anger management. While many of the findings have been acceptable to Christians, some have not. Even some Christian counselors have espoused concepts that other Christians have rejected. Most Christians rightfully insist that a theological view of anger management must be part of the equation.

Christian psychologist Archibald D. Hart talks about the key to managing anger. "I believe that forgiveness is the New Testament's answer to the problem of anger. The concept of forgiveness holds out the most promise for aiding us in effectively resolving anger feelings once they have arisen. Forgiveness is at the heart of the Christian gospel. It is the genius of Christianity, and not without reason. God knows who and what we are, and He has both given and demonstrated forgiveness in a re-markable way. He knows that we need forgiveness, both for receiving it ourselves, as well as for us to give to oth-ers. . . . As a psychologist, I am convinced that to know both how to receive and give forgiveness is crucial to the problem of anger" (*Feeling Free* [Old Tappan, N.J.: Fleming H. Revell, 1979], pp. 69, 77).

Ella found forgiveness to be the key to unlocking anger that kept her from enjoying a relationship with her aunt. She had been nursing anger for 15 years because of something the woman had said to her. When I gave devotional talks to the staff of a Florida hospital, Ella was in the audience. The second day I told the group that forgiveness has the power to end senseless resentment.

The next day she told me, "I practiced what you spoke about yesterday. Gathering my family together, including my aunt, I explained that life is too short to waste by holding grudges. I apologized for the way I behaved and told my aunt that I forgave her for her cutting words 15 years earlier. My aunt hugged me and said that she had never stopped loving me. Our family is now close. We're going to be a real family. You're right. Forgiveness dissolves anger and brings people together."

God gave Ella the gift of forgiveness. He convicted her of the need to forgive, then gave her the courage and the desire to put that gift to work.

When people tell me that they can't find it in themselves to forgive, I give the same answer. "Of course you can't. Forgiveness is not an innate human quality. A quality that God alone possesses, it is His gift to us. We forgive others when His forgiveness fills and overflows from a grateful heart."

I discovered that the key to handling anger is carefully woven into Jesus' Beatitudes. By meditating on this part of His Sermon on the Mount we will learn how to use the key. Consider the first beatitude.

"Blessed are the poor in spirit, for theirs is the kingdom of heaven" (Matt. 5:3).

"You're blessed when you're at the end of your rope. With less of you there is more of God and his rule" (Message).

"Happy are those who know they are spiritually

poor; the Kingdom of heaven belongs to them!" (TEV).

One of my sons loves astronomy. He takes his fine telescope outside on a clear night and loses track of time when he views the heavenly bodies. I have accompanied him several times. We discuss the ever-expanding universe of galaxies and its incomprehensible distances. My six-foot height is nothing compared to the ocean of heavenly lights. I am a mere speck in the vast expanse of space.

Standing in the presence of Jesus via studying the Bible gives me the same feeling of insignificance. His flawless character, gentle spirit, and open acceptance of everyone dwarf me spiritually. I look at my broken life and realize that I have disappointed my Lord. I can't boast of any virtues. Convicted of my deficiencies, I acknowledge my sinful condition.

As I focus on God's goodness I notice the "log" in my own eye (see Matt. 7:3-5). Realizing that God is the only one who can remove it, I kneel in sorrow at Jesus' feet and confess my moral nakedness. As I explore the Scriptures I discover that I'm not alone in my feelings of insignificance.

The prophet Isaiah had a vision in which he entered God's presence. He cried out, "Woe is me, for I am ruined! Because I am a man of unclean lips" (Isa. 6:5). Coming before God, he felt all of his character flaws become glaringly apparent. Standing before the Master, he saw his own weakness.

The apostle Paul met Jesus along a roadway. His self-righteousness showed up like dye on stolen money. Thereafter he called himself the chief of sinners. He taught the infant church that the covering holiness of Jesus is the only acceptable garment.

Every summer for the past eight years I have attended a woodworking show. There I met an artist who creates elaborate wall hangings out of wood. He makes delicate figures by using various blades on a scroll saw. Seeing my interest, he challenged me to try it.

I bought a scroll saw and created a few items, then returned to the show the following year. The artisan had a display of his best work and was in the process of producing another masterpiece. As I watched him, I felt embarrassed at my own lame efforts. Any pride I had nurtured in my handiwork vanished as I stood in the presence of a craftsperson who had been doing it for 20 years.

When I told him about my feeble efforts, he smiled and said, "Don't feel bad. We all have trouble when we are beginning. Let me show you some of the things I have learned." He placed his safety glasses back on his face and shared methods that I had not been able to discover through reading books.

As we come into the presence of the Master and Creator, the source of holiness, we cannot help but feel small and insignificant. The apostle Paul said we have no reason to boast.

Another time I visited a musician in Dorr County, Wisconsin. When he ushered me into his home, I noticed a basket full of ocarinas of various shapes and sizes. I had really come to see his handmade Irish harps, but the ocarinas caught my attention. After all, I had been playing the instrument for several years.

"Let me show you my collection," he offered. "I have an ocarina I'm sure you have never seen." Picking up a wooden one with two holes to blow into at once, he promptly played a delightful classical duet. "Now I'll play a very rare ocarina," he said with a curious expression on his face. From another room he brought a wooden ocarina with three holes to blow into at once and played a trio!

Since then, whenever I play my ocarinas I can hear his duet and trio in my mind. I realize that my journey toward professional ocarina playing has only just begun. That's not all. Whenever I hear another beginner struggling to produce a tune, I can identify with them.

A pastor suggested when I was a boy that I spend time each day studying the life of Jesus. I didn't know the reason at the time. Now I realize that beholding the Savior helps me recognize my own spiritual poverty. Such realization is basic to forgiving others, because it opens the channel to receive God's eternally flowing forgiveness.

The second beatitude shows the logical result of sensing our own spiritual poverty. "Blessed are those who mourn, for they shall be comforted" (Matt. 5:4). Some Bible commentators use this beatitude to show that God comforts those who mourn the loss of a valuable relationship. I have no doubt about God's comfort during grief, but the first beatitude appears to be speaking about the spiritual life, therefore the mourning of this beatitude has to do with our awareness of our spiritual poverty.

As I measure my life by the perfect one of Jesus, I find myself woefully lacking. The realization that I have broken the heart of God by my self-centeredness shatters my own heart. I mourn for my own stubborn resistance to God's eternal love. Sadness overtakes me when I think how I have wasted the resources of unselfish love.

In spite of my lost opportunities to enjoy God's love, He leads me to repent and confess my rebellion. That confession removes the blockage that keeps God's eternal forgiveness from flooding into my soul. The realization that He has washed away my sins brings extreme comfort. Jesus takes away my shame and guilt. I may still regret certain actions, but I have no doubt about pardon from the Supreme Forgiver. This certainty means that I will not moan about not being able to forgive myself. The comfort of total forgiveness paves the way for the experience of the third beatitude: "Blessed are the gentle, for they shall inherit the earth" (verse 5).

Gentleness is possible because the gift of God's forgiveness floods my life with calm. Inner turmoil ceases. Bitterness, resentment, and harbored anger get laid to rest. Such gentleness within the life produces gentleness toward others.

The forgiven person has dropped the last vestige of self, opening their life to the tranquility of the Holy Spirit. He sets about transforming the inner life from anxiety to peace, from worry to assurance, and from touchiness and irritability to gentleness.

Henri J. M. Nouwen described a woman being admitted to a psychiatric hospital. She wore nothing but a dirty thin dress, and both of her hands had curled into tight fists. The orderlies, suspecting contraband, pried open her fingers. Each hand held a coin. For her, to lose them was to forfeit the last vestige of self. Nouwen pictures sinners coming to God with clenched fists, needing to empty their hands of the last vestige of self. Then they could extend those empty hands to God for Him to fill with His gentleness, mercy, kindness, and love. Only after such an experience can we pour those gifts into the hearts of both those we love and the hearts of those who have offended us. The calm, gentle person has the resources to soothe troubled relationships. If we enjoy the peace that exceeds all human understanding, we will exude peace even in the midst of chaos.

I like the story of the disciples of Jesus on the stormy Sea of Galilee (see Mark 4:35-41), because I have a fear of the ocean. Once I took a whale-watching boat at Bar Harbor, Maine, that went 26 miles out from shore. Only the excitement of seeing many humpbacks distracted me from my apprehension of the deep. The disciples were veteran sailors, but they became panic stricken during the storm. They feared they would drown. All the while

Jesus remained in the back of the boat—sleeping! Finally awakening Him, with wide-eyed fear they yelled, "Don't you care that we are perishing?"

In a calm yet commanding voice Jesus said, "Peace be still." The waves calmed into ripples. When our hearts are troubled by sin and there seems to be little hope, we behold the Savior of mercy and pardon. We cry out our confession, and He stills the troubled sea of the soul. He declares, "Blessed are the gentle, the calm, the meek."

Forgiveness is a constant process in person to person situations. Throughout life we will always find some offense to forgive. Even single incidents of provocation can sometimes require time to completely forgive. For this reason the Christian daily seeks God's power to forgive others.

And as we do so we constantly find ourselves astonished at God's eternal forgiveness. We long to enjoy an ever-increasing supply of His goodness. Although life without revenge and resentment can be a rich one, without God's grace we are too spiritually poverty-stricken to make peace with others. The fourth beatitude says, "Blessed are those who hunger and thirst for righteousness, for they shall be satisfied" (Matt. 5:6).

"You're blessed when you've worked up a good appetite for God. He's food and drink in the best meal you'll ever eat" (Message).

"Happy are those whose greatest desire is to do what God requires; God will satisfy them fully!" (TEV).

The highest peak in the Christian journey, this beatitude allows us to gain perspective on life's provocations. Here is where we learn how to decide what we will allow to upset us, how we will respond, and how we will find the best chance of reconciliation. Spending time on this spiritual elevation provides opportunity to make a good choice that will benefit both offended and offender.

Jesus used the words "hunger" and "thirst" to describe the nature of the longing we should have for righteousness. This suggests to me a strong urge to receive the necessary strength to be victorious over inappropriate anger behavior. God forgives us, but He also empowers us to follow His example. When we experience the joy of forgiven-ness and forgiving-ness, we want to continue tasting that joy.

This makes sense to me because I have an appetite for cornbread that has not waned since my boyhood. My Pennsylvania Dutch mother made cornbread and cornmeal mush using Brinser's toasted cornmeal. The corn is roasted golden brown before being ground into meal. When you open the bag, the meal smells exactly like freshly popped corn. Cornbread made with this flour has the same aroma. My family has moved to Ohio, Connecticut, Massachusetts, Michigan, Texas, and Arkansas, but we never run out of Brinser's cornmeal. We have it shipped to our home wherever we live. Every Friday evening we have soup and cornbread and apple butter for supper. I never lose my appetite for this delicacy. If we have any left over from supper, I eat it for breakfast the next morning.

That's the way it is with God's righteousness, grace, and power to keep relationships healthy. Once you've tasted it, you desire more and more.

D. Martyn Lloyd-Jones summarized this beatitude. "To hunger and thirst after righteousness is to desire to be free from self in all its horrible manifestations, in all its forms. When we considered the man who is meek, we saw that all that really means is that he is free from self in its every shape and form—self-concern, pride, boasting, self-protection, sensitiveness, always imagining people are against him, a desire to protect self and glorify self" (*Studies in the Sermon on the Mount* [Grand Rapids: Eerdmans, 1959], p. 79).

Lloyd-Jones' comments may sound a bit negative but he is really saying that freedom from a self-centered life gives liberty to enjoy wholeness. We are free to forgive without hesitation.

In my book *God's Gift of Forgiveness* I suggested that the first four beatitudes describe the emptying of self so as to allow God to fill us with His grace. But then He gives us so much grace that it overflows to others, blessing them. Beatitudes five, six, and seven describe our attitudes toward others as a result of being filled to overflowing.

I learned to swim in a spring-fed lake near Fredericksburg, Pennsylvania. The sun warmed only the surface of the water. If you dive deep into it you will feel the frigid water welling up from the springs at the bottom of the lake. As your body moves through the water you can feel the fluctuations of cool and cooler. Swishing through the water is invigorating on a sultry summer day.

The secret of the lake's appeal is the springs and the steady flow of water over the spillway. Contrast this with the lake at Cleburne State Park in Texas, one fed by rain runoff. During the persistent heat of summer the water never reaches the spillway. The temperature of the water is like that of bathwater, and slippery mud covers the bottom of the lake. There is no overflow and no refreshing.

Sinners who receive the gift of God's eternal forgiveness overflow with blessings to others. Directed by the Holy Spirit, they will show mercy to those unkind to them. They will be sincere in their desire to restore relationships, and they will be peacemakers under all circumstances.

Some Christians struggle with forgiveness. They have the idea that they must forgive others before God will forgive them. But such a works-oriented mentality isn't logical. It is only when I have realized my own spiritual poverty and opened my life to God's eternal forgiveness that I have anything to give to others. When

God forgives me, part of the gift includes the desire to be considerate, sympathetic, and merciful to others.

Forgiveness is a way of life for the Christian. In 1943 Uwe Holmer was an enthusiastic member of Hitler Youth. Soon he became interested in joining the SS because they were tough soldiers who fought to the bitter end. Then his mother noticed an SS publication in his room. When she confronted him, he admitted that joining the SS was his dream. She asked him a question that would stay with him. "They are the ones who shoot prisoners and Jews. Is that the sort of organization you want to live and die for?"

Near the end of the war Hitler had 15-year-olds drafted into military service. Uwe's chapter of Hitler Youth volunteered for the SS—100 of them. But, remembering his mother's question, he refused even in the face of ridicule.

After the war he married and became a pastor at Lobetal, a suburb of East Berlin. He founded a Christian community for epileptic and mentally disabled adults. For years the East German government of Erich Honecker constantly harassed him. Eight times its Ministry of Education, headed by Margot Honecker, denied the admission of the Holmer children into a university. Then in 1989 the Berlin Wall fell, and Honecker fled office as one of the most hated men in Europe. He and his family found themselves evicted from their luxurious palace in Vandlitz. But the Holmers welcomed them into their home. Protesters sent death threats and created havoc in front of their house, but forgiveness prevailed. Pastor Holmer reported that although the Honeckers did not renounce their atheism, they folded their hands and bowed their heads when the family prayed together. I am sure that the experience had an effect on Honecker before his death.

The overflow of grace, peace, forgiveness, and joy will refresh those within the community of faith. When the family of faith squabbles about worship styles and other minor issues, it indicates that they have ceased to be astonished at the unconditional and free-flowing stream of God's forgiveness. When astonishment withers, the overflow stops. And when the overflow halts within the faith family, those outside the family receive nothing. Robert Farrar Capon observes that "the heart of Christian astonishment is the mind-boggling goodness of the good news" (*The Astonished Heart* [Grand Rapids: Eerdmans, 1996], p. 16).

Forgiveness is cause for enthusiasm and celebration. Our son was working at a Christian summer camp. As he was walking to the boating dock, a 10-year-old girl ran after him. "Steve! Steve! Guess what! I gave my heart to Jesus!" What astonishment! That feeling can be ours if we experience the beatitudes every day. Others will benefit from our astonishment overflow.

Unfortunately, too many neglect the eighth beatitude: "Blessed are those who have been persecuted for the sake of righteousness, for theirs is the kingdom of heaven. Blessed are you when people insult you and persecute you, and falsely say all kinds of evil against you because of Me" (Matt. 5:10, 11).

Jesus made it clear that if we follow Him, we will also share in His suffering. We will be offended, insulted, and hated just as He was. Because of that, we will need His strength to say as He did, "Father, forgive them."

All of us at times meet situations that make it difficult to forgive. That's when we are thankful for the privilege to retrace our steps on the journey to heaven. We will acknowledge our spiritual poverty, open ourselves to God's free pardon, receive the calm and peace of renewal, and once again stand on the pinnacle of grace where God assuages our thirst and hunger for His righteousness. On this pinnacle we gain perspective and power to handle even the most difficult situations.

Our sons and I backpacked in Pigeon River Country State Forest in Michigan five years in succession. One year we snaked our way through dense tree-covered trails. A bit confused about finding our way back to the base camp, we came to a fire tower, climbed to the top, and surveyed the forest spread out before us. In a few minutes we knew exactly how to make our way back.

The first four beatitudes are like a tower we climb every day. Daily we renew our relationship with God and receive insight and strength for meeting life's provocations. We gain the ability to make the wisest choices about how to react or whether even to respond at all.

When we forgive we are participating with Jesus in His work of redemption. By allowing His forgiveness to flow to us, in us, and through us, we become conduits of His love. Jesus said that by His crucifixion He would draw all people to Him. He uses those who have been changed by the power of the cross to be part of that magnetic miracle. As the world sees forgiveness breaking down hatred and resentment, they will feel God's drawing power.

# Chapter 9

# FORGIVENESS
# IN THE FAMILY

S atan takes great delight in shattering families. He uses out of control anger, resentment, hatred, and grudge-holding as weapons to destroy the fabric of society. His arsenal seems invincible, not only when we read the divorce notices in the newspaper, but especially when we see families in the church crumbling.

After I conducted a church seminar, the pastor wanted to talk to me in private. He told me that the church pianist had just filed divorce papers against her husband who happened to be an elder in the congregation. Then he described several families riddled with immorality, dishonesty, and long-standing feuds. "I simply don't know where to turn," he said finally.

"Do personal visitation, design seminars dealing with family life, but above all, preach the Gospel," I advised him. "The apostle Paul said he was not ashamed of the Gospel, because it is the power of God for salvation to everyone who believes."

Psychologist John White is saddened by the tendency of pastors to look to psychology to solve perplexing family problems in the church. "We expect too much of psychology. And we do so in part because we have lost confidence in the Christian gospel, however much we profess to believe it. Consequently, we are too prone to pass on difficult cases to obliging counselors, social workers and psychologists without carefully considering whether we are doing so merely to get rid of a problem we ought to have been able to solve. . . . Christianity has not been tried and found wanting—it has been found but not really tried, even by the churches. Only an emasculated, gutless travesty of it has been tried" (*Putting the Soul Back in Psychology* [Downers Grove, Ill.: InterVarsity Press, 1987], pp. 59-67).

The overarching reality of the gospel is forgiveness. Forgiveness has great power. It can take a family in total chaos and create from it a sanctuary in which one can sense and welcome God's presence. A forgiven family can heal oozing wounds and restore broken relationships.

The gospel is bad news to Satan because it is the anti-ballistic missile that can intercept his warheads before they strike the home. It can reconstruct families already in ruins. And it can fortify the family so that it is impregnable against the wiles of Satan.

A church-going man who had a form of godliness but didn't live a God-centered life ruled his large family with an iron fist. When the children grew to adulthood, they all left the church, because he had never taught them the true meaning of the gospel. They did not see the love, tenderness, and forgiveness of God lived in the home, but eventually the power of the gospel—the power of forgiveness—did change their family. Today they worship God in the same church. The father is still working on some of the rough spots that drove his children from the church, but the power of forgiveness is willing to wait for the Lord's remodeling process to iron out the remaining wrinkles in his character.

I know several couples who went through a divorce and then let the Holy Spirit convict them to open their life to God's forgiveness. They gave forgiveness to each other and remarried. Can you imagine how such turnarounds must have upset Satan?

God has a great affection for the family. He created the very first one, provided its members with an unspoiled home, and visited with them every day. The Bible doesn't record how long God ambled through their garden home with them before sin entered their Eden abode. The Genesis story just tells about the day when the daily walks ceased.

The remainder of the book of Genesis records the history of family turmoil characterized by trickery, fraud, dishonesty, infidelity, and revenge. Tucked into the history every now and then we read about the fresh breezes of forgiveness that brought harmony into the family, but those examples seem to be so scarce. Yet lying beneath the biblical history is the aquifer of God's eternal forgiveness waiting for His chosen people to tap into it, waiting to restore the families twisted by self-centeredness and the lack of commitment.

By the time we arrive at the book of Exodus, the families of Israel had been in slavery and spiritual darkness for hundreds of years. The pagan practices of Egypt had diluted the holiness of their families, but yet the springs of God's forgiveness remained fresh, flowing, and awaiting their reception. God used Moses to teach them the gospel. Through stunning miracles the Lord redeemed the families of Israel, saving then from a slavery much more devastating than their drudgery in the brickyards.

Many Christians believe the plagues were God's way of convincing the pharaoh to release the Israelites, but a number of scholars have an additional view. Some in Israel may have come to believe in the Egyptians' gods. The display of miracles offered proof beyond the shadow of a doubt that there is only one God—the Creator and

Redeemer. The plagues demonstrated that the so-called gods of Egypt were powerless.

Just before God opened the way out of Egypt, God invited all the families of Israel to sprinkle a lamb's blood on their doorposts and eat a meal together. That first Passover acted out the truth of forgiveness in every family. The blood of the lamb redeemed them. The ocean of God's forgiveness flooded the homes of Israel before the opening of the sea that had trapped them.

Shortly after the Red Sea mud dried from their sandals, the people gathered near Mount Sinai and listened to Moses deliver a message of encouragement. "God told me that you are a covenant people, His own possession," their leader declared. Then he ascended the mountain and received the Ten Commandments. The preamble that God spoke gave the context of the commandments. "I am the Lord your God, who brought you out of the land of Egypt, out of the house of slavery" (Ex. 20:2). God couched the law in the reality of redemption.

It is interesting that God presented the Ten Commandments *after* He had redeemed Israel from slavery. Could this suggest that living out the law of God is the *result* of redemption rather than a way of earning it?

God intends the commandments to be a guide to wholeness and holiness. Each promises and confirms holiness. And each has a bearing on the solidarity of the family. The grace and forgiveness of God precedes everything that comprises a whole and holy family.

*You shall have no other gods before Me.* God is holy.

*You shall not make for yourself an idol.* Worship is holy.

*You shall not take the name of the Lord your God in vain.* Prayer is holy.

*Remember the Sabbath day to keep it holy.* Time and work are holy.

*Honor your father and your mother.* Family is holy.

*You shall not murder.* Life is holy.
*You shall not commit adultery.* Sex and intimacy is holy.
*You shall not steal.* Matter is holy.
*You shall not bear false witness.* Language is holy.
*You shall not covet.* Your neighbor is holy.

Clearly the bedrock of a happy family is acknowledging the holiness of God, worshiping and communicating with Him during His holy day and throughout the workweek. Instead of talking *about* God, the unified family talks *to* God and *with* Him. Without this holy foundation the family can crumble when difficult times come.

Elliott Currie wrote a most disturbing book, *The Road to Whatever,* that documents the erosion of solidarity in the homes of middle-class America. Currie talks about the inversion of responsibility that forces adolescents to grow up on their own. Mothers and fathers increasingly focus on their respective careers, are gone 24/7, and thus have no time to spend with family. It is what Eugene Peterson calls the desecration of holy time. Anger and resentment fester in the hearts of such teenagers. With no training in the skills of conflict management and forgiveness they get involved in self-destructive behavior.

"One of the most common laments among troubled middle-class youth," Currie writes, "is that they were saddled with too much responsibility for managing their lives as they were growing up. They experienced childhood and adolescence not as a time when they were 'brought up' in any meaningful sense by competent and admirable adults but as one when they had to figure out how to navigate life on their own" ([New York: Henry Holt and Company, 2004], pp. 48, 49). He interviewed many adolescents who were actually discarded by their parents, something we assumed happened only in lower-class families. After being kicked out by parents, many teens lived with the families of friends until they were again asked to leave. From there many slid deeper into self-destructive behavior.

In the absence of family time it is no wonder that teenagers do not view family as holy. Home deteriorates to nothing more than a motel in which relationships are shallow, and resentment, hatred, and toxic language are the norm. It provides no time for a family meal, let alone attending to spiritual needs. Such youth consequently do not learn that life, intimacy, and others are holy. They take "the road to whatever," not caring about consequences. But it is a road far from the plan that God gave to Israel.

I can picture an Israelite mother and father gathering their children for evening worship. Reviewing the Ten Commandments, they teach their children how they make their family strong. They tell the children that their forgiving God who redeemed them comes first in everything. Their God is a God of right priorities, which if always kept will keep their family together.

The children of Israel knew that their entire life was based on forgiveness. God asked Moses to build a sanctuary—a God-with-us house. Forgiveness was the central motif in the services of that holy place. The priests explained confession, sacrifice, and restoration as worshipers came before the Lord. Any act of unkindness or provocation could be resolved before the sun went down on anger. The daily offering in the tabernacle provided the assurance that the penitent was able to live free of guilt.

Every morning during Israel's sojourn in the wilderness a shade-producing cloud followed the families. Every night a fire-pillar did the same. The families knew that their Forgiver was always present. If they ever doubted the availability of power to forgive and love, they needed only to look out of their tent.

God desired to write His commands in the minds of every member of the Israelite community. He intended for them to be the community of the forgiven and forgiving. In their deepest consciousness God wanted them to remember that He is holy, worship is holy, talking and listening to Him are holy, time and work are holy, life is holy, intimacy is holy, material things are holy, language is holy, and the neighbor is holy.

Unfortunately, family life deteriorated in Israel just as it has in the twenty-first century. It became twisted and full of anger, revenge, and toxic behavior. The miracles of creation and redemption became dim in their minds until they no longer celebrated their deliverance.

Israel's eventual collapse should be a lesson to those who claim that God's law has been abrogated. If you tear away the commandments, you rip out the very heart of family harmony. Throwing them away opens the way for disrespect for God, nature, time, family, life, and others. It encourages family members to live just for themselves.

Love for God and love for others are the two pillars of His Ten Commandments. The first four pertain to our relationship with Him while the last six relate to our dealings with others. I was intrigued at the location of the commandment to keep family holy—to honor father and mother. If one command hinges on the previous one, we find an interesting concept. Treating the essentials of life as holy would be something learned in the family. The family would teach all how to handle provocation, how to make wise decisions about how to respond to offence, and how to forgive others. And the family would then be the nursery that cultivates forgiveness so that it can be transplanted outside the home.

When I was in college one of the young men living in the dormitory with me frequently drove a new car. All of us were envious, but we also sensed that something about him was not on the level. One day two federal marshals entered the dormitory and asked for the room number of the fellow with the fancy cars. When they knocked on his door, he refused to open. The marshals kicked the door open, handcuffed our dorm mate, and took him to prison. He had been stealing cars and selling them across the state line. A few weeks later the dean invited the marshals to speak to all of us.

They told us that most crimes are committed by people who didn't learn in the home to respect their own property, let alone that of others. Their remarks confirm in my mind the importance of learning forgiveness and life values in the home. Once we can discover how to forgive in the home we will then practice it outside the home.

A family asked me to meet with them. Longstanding disagreements and resentments were interfering with the proper care of their dying mother. Some of the children refused to visit the mother because she lived with a sibling they disliked. The primary caregiver was upset because the whole burden of care rested on her shoulders. And the mother in the back bedroom knew that her children were not getting along.

First of all, I invited them to talk about their experience growing up together. It brought to mind good memories and created laughter and a few tears. They hadn't done that for years. Although they remembered little squabbles, like those of any family, they also discussed how they had resolved their differences.

Then I told them that they were simply children who had grown a bit older. I suggested that the techniques used to resolve childhood differences would probably still work. One by one they confessed their faults, spoke words of forgiveness, and worked out a plan to care for their mother. When I left the home, they all went to their mother's room and told her that her children had stopped fighting. News of the forgiveness elevated her spirits and allowed her to spend her last weeks of life in peace.

Forgiveness is *taught* and *caught* in the family. Small children often get into scraps with other children. Parents can use such occasions to teach forgiveness. It is not wise to force a child to apologize and forgive, because you never want them to view apology and forgiveness as punishments. But parents can suggest that it is worth thinking about. They might talk about the happy times their children would miss by holding a grudge, and then allow them to think about it and follow through with action of their own.

Experts in child development suggest that we can teach forgiveness and conflict resolution by reading stories to children. Such stories should approach the subject in a positive manner, not like the kind of bedtime stories our boys disliked. In them children who disobeyed or were unkind received a spanking. The author never used the word "spanked," but alluded to it so that our sons knew what had happened. Recent authors of children's books address many situations in a very tasteful way.

Divorce often turns into a struggle between parents. It is obvious to the children that forgiveness is not happening, and they may even feel that they should not forgive either. They learn to nurse anger because their parents are modeling such behavior so well. Judith Wallerstein's research revealed that children of divorce remain angry for years at one or both parents for destroying their secure home. Their unwillingness to forgive gets caught from their parents. Anger and resentment often intensifies when children shuttle back and forth from one home to another, often against their wishes.

One of my jobs as a child was to walk the half-mile down the farm lane to bring the mail and newspaper from the mailbox. I often stopped along the way to watch a bumblebee or butterfly. Sometimes I practiced my harmonica where nobody could hear my mistakes. Hearing a rustling in the cornfield beside the lane one day, I quickly jumped into the tall weeds alongside it and peered out at the noise. I saw my great Uncle Lou filling a sack with my father's corn. It horrified me to learn that Uncle Lou was a thief. When he disappeared with his sack full of corn, I ran home to tell my father.

Although I expected my father to be shocked and angry just as I was, he wasn't. "Well, Bubs," he commented, "I don't think Uncle Lou's few hens will eat enough corn to make a dent in a 40-acre field. It would have been nice of him to ask, but maybe he didn't have time to come all the way to the house to ask permission."

I was only 8 when that happened, but I still remember my father's forgiving spirit. He didn't lecture me about forgiveness—he simply lived it. I hope I caught that same spirit.

As one of eight siblings, I learned the value of forgiveness in the home when I was growing up. We had our differences, but we stuck up for each other when one of us was in trouble. When school bullies were stealing my coat and pushing me down a steep bank, my brother took me to the home of the justice of the peace. The officer asked me to tell him the names of the bullies and describe their actions. Going to my school, he called each of the boys out of class. Then he warned them that if they bullied me one more time, he would take each of them to where their respective fathers worked and would request each father to punish in the customary fashion. Thanks to my brother's loyalty, that was the end of the bullying.

The atmosphere of our home was a blessing to underprivileged and abused children. The YMCA of Philadelphia sent what they called "sunshine kids" to our farm for the summer. The acceptance and warmth of our family was a healing tonic for children who lived in a hostile environment. By the end of the summer they didn't want to go home.

Forgiveness in the family is evangelism at its best. Demonstrating forgiveness is superior to proclaiming it. Put the two together, and you have a real heart appeal.

One time as I listened to Eugene H. Peterson speak to a large audience, he announced that he wasn't going to talk about the gospel because we had heard it many times before. He said it is easier to keep on learning more and more and put off the living part of the gospel. Instead, we need to start living what we've already learned about forgiveness.

When a family is living forgiveness, such a family becomes the light on the lamp stand that Jesus spoke about. Others look at such a family and say to themselves, "If they can live in harmony, I think I'd like to find out what makes them like that."

When I was working my way through school, I was one of the janitors of a church in West Philadelphia. Although I was only 16 and wasn't the perfect workman, I diligently tried to keep the church building spotless. The janitorial supply salespeople taught me how to clean toilets and strip and wax floors. I thought I was making progress, but I must have been inattentive to details. A woman who had financial influence in the congregation ran her white glove over the top of a doorframe. I failed her test. She went to the church board and had me released from the job.

Fortunately, a man who believed in forgiveness and practiced it in his home came to my rescue. Since he was also a peacemaker, he saw no value in confronting the influential matriarch of the church. Instead he drove me to his house once a week. Giving me little jobs around the house and yard, he paid me the same amount that I had been earning at the church. He expressed his appreciation for my work and told me that he believed in me. That happened 50 years ago, but I still remember the tasty meals, the kind words, and his forgiving spirit.

In a previous chapter I told about Ella who forgave her aunt and brought harmony into her family. That transformation spilled over into her community. Once she stood in the checkout line at the grocery store with a full shopping cart. A man behind her began swearing and acting rudely. Instead of being offended she turned and said, "Sir, you must have an urgent appointment. Why don't you go ahead of me?" The man thanked her. Just behind the first man was another irritated man. "Sir, you come ahead of me," she said to him. "I'm not as busy as you are."

"I always wondered what in the world I could do for God," Ella later told me. "Now I know that I can be forgiving and show kindness." She had discovered how to participate in God's work of redemption.

Every family should be a buffer zone. The world can be very harsh and unbending. Stresses can be enormous. Employers don't always overlook mistakes, and their expectations can be unrealistic. Coming home should be like entering an oasis after a long trip in the desert heat.

Family should also be a place in which to grow. Learning to relate to each other inevitably causes pain, but forgiveness gives us a chance to begin again. We learn to love and appreciate each other in an atmosphere of trust.

A family is more likely to be forgiving if it incorporates the following principles.

*Time Together*—Come together to celebrate birthdays and other special occasions. For example, when a child turns 12, or some age significant to your family, gather for a meal and a blessing. Each member of the family can write a blessing and read it to the child. Help each other with projects. Enjoy the outdoors together. Attend musical concerts. Play games, especially ones outdoors. Avoid the couch-potato activity of television viewing, because it stifles interaction.

*Communication*—Get beyond talking about weather. Share ideas important to you. Express positive feelings, and listen to others when they reveal their feelings. In times of loss and other difficulties, acknowledge the pain and be present for the hurting family member.

*Commitment*—Make a vow to love and respect every member of your family. Be sure to resolve any differences quickly and without rancor.

*Appreciation and Affirmation*—Determine that you will not take any family member for granted. Write thank-you notes even though you may live close. When a person does something well or achieves a goal, let him or her know that you are proud of them.

*Spiritual Health*—By this I do not mean that you pressure other family members to practice faith the way you do. Just make sure that your personal relationship with God is strong. Continually and daily follow the Beatitude approach to spiritual health as outlined in this book.

*Through Eyes of Possibility*—We all make mistakes and sometimes ruffle feathers the wrong way. Every family experiences this. The important approach to those who offend is to see them through the eyes of possibility. God looks at us and sees what we can become through His grace. He can help us to view others the same way.

*Learn to Manage Conflict*—Books and adult education programs that teach the principle of conflict management are very helpful. Some families have occasional family meetings or reunions that incorporate affirmation and appreciation activities.

I see these components of a happy family as preventive measures that keep it open to building relationships instead of just taking them for granted.

For 10 years I lived among 52 Amish families. I have worshiped with them, gone to their weddings and school graduations, helped them make hay, assisted them in building, and took them shopping. On several occasions I have accompanied them on long trips and stayed in their homes overnight. In the process I have eaten in their homes, played table games with them in the evening, and joined them for community singing. I was curious to know why they appeared to enjoy such family solidarity.

Like any family, they experience differences of opinion, occasional conflicts, and even violations of their lifestyle, but a spirit of forgiveness prevails among the Amish community and within its various family units. I have concluded that several factors contribute to their spirit of forgiveness and unanimity. First, they live by the principle of interdependence. A construction accident injured my neighbor. Families from miles around mowed his hay and stored it in his barn. When a young mother of three became ill a large group of women planted her garden. Another group of young wives gathered at their respective homes to weed their gardens, share recipes, and make crafts to sell in support of their school. Three different families cared for a hospitalized mother's children so the father could plant his crops.

The same interdependence exists in the family unit itself. When the children earn money doing jobs outside the home, a portion of it helps with household expenses and another portion gets saved for the young person's future needs. This arrangement does not upset the young.

Another factor that contributes to family peace is taking time for family togetherness. Twice a week the young people have games. Parents assist in them. Every other Sunday evening one of the homes serves a large meal followed by singing. Families work together. My neighbor had three small children. One spring day I noticed the husband sowing alfalfa seed in a field of newly planted oats. His wife was sitting on the ground next to the bag of seed while the children played in the dirt. I noticed that during church the fathers care for small children as frequently as the mothers. It is common to see a father raking hay with a child seated next to him. Contrary to what some misinformed authors say, Amish parents for the most part are not harsh or authoritarian.

A major difference arose between two Amish neighbors. One of them suggested to the other that a third party meet with them to help restore the relationship, but that was not necessary. The offending neighbor came to the home of the family he had injured and said, "I owe your family an apology. I have been a man who has to have his own way, but that is not a good attitude. I have asked God to help me change. I'm very sorry for the pain I have caused your family."

A young mother severely burned in a propane gas explosion lived only for a few days before she died. Many of the families traveled more than an hour to attend the funeral and support her family.

Amish homes have a spiritual tone that engenders peace and gentleness. When the family has gathered around the dinner table, the father gives a quiet signal, and everyone, including babies, bows their head for silent prayer. After the meal they have another silent prayer. At their worship services the entire family sits quietly for almost three hours for singing and preaching. Their homes and religious assemblies have a special reverence.

One morning I took my neighbor to town for an item to fix something that his son had broken. It was an expensive repair. The father quietly told me that he had made his own share of foolish mistakes when he was young. He was sure that his son would learn an important lesson from this one. His calmness and spirit of forgiveness amazed me. Years later I met that son, now 20. Although harassed by the men on the construction crew on which he worked, he would just laugh and show no animosity toward the men. He had learned to manage anger from his father.

My family and I have also experienced their concern. One winter I struggled with a serious case of bronchitis. Early in the morning I went to the bathroom to spray medication on my inflamed throat. At daylight my Amish neighbor called me. "Larry, are you OK? When we went to milk the cows at 4:00 this morning we saw the light shining in your bathroom window."

I learned from the Amish that the groundwork for a home that abundantly practices forgiveness is laid by a life of simplicity and a deep relationship with the Master Forgiver. Developing forgiveness in the family must be intentional. It is folly to assume that it can be acquired without hard work and total reliance on the Giver of all good gifts.

# Chapter 10

# A CLOSER LOOK
# AT FORGIVENESS

R ecently forgiveness has become a topic for research. The first National Conference on
Forgiveness took place under the auspices of the
University of Wisconsin-Madison in 1995. Archbishop
Desmond Tutu opened the conference by saying, "No
one can be fully human unless he or she relates to others
in a fair, peaceful, and harmonious way. . . . Anything
that subverts this harmony is injurious, not just to the
community but [to] all of us, and therefore forgiveness is
an absolute necessity for continued human existence.
The world is on the brink of disaster if we don't forgive,
accept forgiveness, and reconcile" (in Robert D. Enright
and Joanna North, eds., *Exploring Forgiveness* [Madison,
Wis.: University of Wisconsin Press, 1998], pp. xiii-xvi).

Prior to such recent studies very little had been written about interpersonal forgiveness. From the early fifth
century to 1970 only one literary work had appeared
about every 15 years. While the growing interest in the
topic is encouraging, some researchers are troubled about
the focus on the strictly self-benefits of forgiveness. We
notice this in much of the self-help literature that claims
that forgiveness is something you do for yourself and not
as a gift to the offender as well. This emphasis slices for-

giveness in half, destroying, I believe, its essential quality.

Another view that concerns some researchers is the belief that wrong-doing is not the primary cause of pain. Rather, it is our perception of the situation that triggers it. This philosophy maintains that our job is to change our viewpoint to the exclusion of acknowledging the wrong done against us. Specialists in forgiveness think this may work for minor offences but not for extreme injustices.

Everett Worthington found that those who forgive solely to benefit themselves will receive only minimal help, but benefit levels remained high for those who forgave to help both victim and perpetrator. He summarized it in this way. "Forgiving seems to be for *giving,* not for getting. . . . Forgiveness does benefit us. But if we forgive mainly to get, we get just a trickle of all those benefits. . . . If we try to bless others by forgiving, then paradoxically we are flooded with blessings ourselves" (*Five Steps to Forgiveness* [New York: Crown Publishers, 2001], pp. 14, 15).

Joanna North wrote, "Forgiveness is not something that we do for ourselves alone, but something that we give or offer to another. The forgiving response is outward-looking and other-directed" (*Exploring Forgiveness,* p. 19).

I experienced the two-way blessings of forgiveness when I was 16. While attending a parochial high school in Philadelphia, I lived in the home of a widow, Mrs. Walters. Three of us boys occupied one large bedroom. Late one Friday night one boy pretended to have a nightmare. He awakened us and chased us around the room with a cane he had found in the closet. The noise awakened Mrs. Walters from a deep sleep, causing her near apoplexy.

The next day the principal told me that Mrs. Walters had decided that I had to leave because I was the oldest boy and supposedly could have prevented the mischief. Moving into the home of a professor, I thereafter avoided Mrs. Walters even though we both attended the same church. I suffered extreme emotional pain because resentment was contrary to the values my parents had instilled in me. Finally, I decided to forgive, if for no other reason than to relieve my own inner turmoil.

I returned to her home with one of the boys still boarding there. When Mrs. Walters entered the living room, I began weeping as I said, "Mrs. Walters, I'm sorry." That motherly saint took me in her arms and said, "I'm so happy you came. I have missed you. I'm sorry this has been so painful for both of us." While forgiveness helped me, it also blessed her. In the coming years she and I would enjoy a rich friendship.

"Forgiveness is about more than feelings. Our emotions are a tremendously important part of who we are. But forgiveness isn't simply about feelings; it's about how we live together, about how we undertake to behave toward one another, about the releasing of old wrongs, the restoration of peace, and the mending of relationships" (L. William Countryman, *Forgiven and Forgiving* [Harrisburg, Pa.: Morehouse Publishing, 1998], p. 9).

But forgiveness can be risky. We have no assurance that the other party will receive us or respond in a positive manner, because forgiveness and reconciliation are not the same. We cannot be reconciled without forgiveness, but we can forgive without reconciliation. Lewis Smedes talked about forgiving for your own sake when the other party is not willing to meet with you, or when it is not safe or possible to make contact.

Ideally, reconciliation should follow forgiveness, but we do not live in an ideal world. Some situations allow forgiveness to go only one way. In that event we can give forgiveness from the heart but not in person. This is necessary to enable us to move into the future without dragging the past behind us.

For decades I have worked with grieving people,

many who were experiencing complicated mourning due to unfinished business. Some harbored grudges and resentments that had not been settled before another person's death. Others wept about deeds of kindness postponed. Unforgiveness plagued their minds and kept them from active grief and adequate adjustment.

I recommended two ways of resolving their conflict. One involved writing a letter to the deceased with either apology or words of forgiveness even though the letter could not reach the person. Pray to God, I suggested, and tell Him what they planned to say to the person in heaven. Verbalizing the apology or words of forgiveness helped many to escape the quagmire of guilt and opened the path to adjustment.

While forgiveness doesn't erase the offense from the mind, it enables us to relate to the memory in a constructive way. Instead of triggering or fueling resentment, the memory reminds us that God's grace has helped us to forgive. We rejoice in victory through the power of Christ.

I emphasized that forgiveness and trust are not the same. Forgiveness is a gift. Trust must be earned. A wife can forgive her husband for infidelity, but her husband needs to demonstrate fidelity, commitment, and love. Such trust will not come easily or quickly.

Andrea forgave her husband for spending long evening hours viewing pornographic material on the Internet, but he continued to work on his computer late at night. When she complained, he said, "If you really forgave me, you'd trust me." He was not willing to earn her trust; neither did he differentiate between it and her forgiveness.

Archbishop Desmond Tutu said that "forgiveness is taking seriously the awfulness of what has happened when you are treated unfairly" (in *Exploring Forgiveness,* p. xiii). It is necessary to determine whether the other person is truly to be blamed or whether you are the one at fault. In cases of extreme injustices and crimes it can be obvious that the other is to blame. We must never associate condoning or excusing wrong-doing with forgiveness. Interpersonal forgiveness requires acknowledging that wrong-doing. And the consequences of such wrong-doing are not eliminated.

Such consequences may mean imprisonment by the legal system, mandated separation from family members, or loss of position. While such results are inevitable, this does not prevent interpersonal forgiveness.

I once read a book written by a woman whose husband received a lengthy sentence for sexually molesting a minor. Because she knew that he would otherwise have no support, she visited him in prison. She forgave him, and he demonstrated willingness to receive the therapy necessary to alleviate the problem. After serving his full sentence and earning her trust, they renewed their marriage vows.

Forgiveness is hard work. It is more difficult to forgive than to hate, but the more we forgive, the easier it becomes. It is a spiritual skill that we learn by exercising it. As we practice the skill, "an attitude of goodwill and moral virtue develops. Forgiveness has a way of transforming your character and relationships as you understand and practice it" (Robert D. Enright, *Forgiveness Is a Choice* [Washington, D.C.: American Psychological Association, 2001], p. 74).

We will have many opportunities to practice forgiveness because we are bound to offend and be offended in our imperfect world. An attitude of forgiveness will smooth the way to keeping our relationships healthy and happy. Forgiveness is the antidote for bitterness. Hebrews 12:14, 15 says, "Follow peace . . . lest any root of bitterness springing up trouble you, and thereby many be defiled" (KJV).

In Texas I watched a farmer clearing a field in preparation for planting milo. Mesquite trees had overgrown the land. They were six to eight feet high, but most of the trees were underground. The farmer had a six-foot long hook attached to the back of his bulldozer. The hook snagged the long branches and roots and dragged them to the surface. I was told that without regular chisel plowing the root fragments left in the ground would soon develop into more mesquite trees. Forgiveness is like the hook on that bulldozer and subsequent chisel plowing. It keeps bitterness from growing and crowding out happiness from personal life, home, church, and community.

Everett Worthington gives five steps to forgiveness. While I question the practicality of following steps, dissecting the process of forgiveness does have value. The following paraphrase of the steps may be helpful.

> **First Step:** Acknowledge that you have been hurt and don't waste time shaking your fist and wishing for an apology that may not happen.
>
> **Second Step:** Brainstorm about what might have caused the person to offend you. Some call this empathy.
>
> **Third Step:** Call upon God for the grace to bestow the gift of forgiveness upon the offender, then thank Him every day for enabling you to forgive.
>
> **Fourth Step:** Deepen your forgiveness by sharing the good news of your experience with a friend.
>
> **Fifth Step:** Enumerate the offender's good qualities and hold on to forgiveness if you should doubt whether you have really forgiven. Realize that the pain of a remembered offense doesn't mean you haven't forgiven (see *Five Steps to Forgiveness* [New York: Crown Publishers, 2001]).

Forgiveness disallows cataloguing offenses for future recall. It refuses to develop an arsenal in case of a future negative situation. R. Lifton Hudson calls this false forgiveness. This is burying the hatchet and then making a map of the burial site, freezing resentment for future thawing, or dropping grudges into a river after teaching the grudges how to swim.

Combing through books about forgiveness I have often noticed chapters that tell readers how to forgive themselves. In emergency rooms I have frequently heard people say, "I will never be able to forgive myself for . . ." For years I tried to analyze the belief that you can forgive yourself. My thoughts became clearer after our son perished in a car-truck accident.

I had bought a Plymouth Satellite from a used car dealer. My son and I repaired the body and made sure the brakes were in proper working order. He drove that car for more than a year with no mishaps. Then one morning on his way to his seminary classes he was killed in that car.

It appeared that the Plymouth stalled when he attempted to enter a highway. The driver of the oncoming truck swerved into the passing lane to miss him, but at that instant our son managed to restart the Plymouth and pulled into the path of the truck. For months I punished myself. I knew from experience that Plymouths of that vintage had a tendency to stall unless the motor was hot. Telling myself that I should never have bought that particular car for him, I believed that I was partly to blame for his death.

Try as I might, I could not forgive myself for my lack of foresight. Thoughts of my poor decision constantly pummeled my mind. Finally, I talked to God about it. I told him about my misery and inability to forgive myself. I asked Him to forgive me for giving our son a Plymouth. Then I thanked Him for forgiving me. Nearly 25 years later I still occasionally thank God for forgiving my poor judgment.

I concluded after searching the Bible that Scripture does not teach or illustrate self-forgiveness. Chuck Lynch observed that the practice of self-forgiveness "unintentionally tends to deify the self as the ultimate granter of forgiveness" (*I Should Forgive, But . . .* [Nashville: Word Publishing, 1998], p. 137). If God is the Ultimate Forgiver, who am I to presume to usurp His position? Besides, forgiveness is interpersonal.

Forgiveness can be researched, dissected, analyzed, and defined, but when it all boils down, it is something that can't be humanly understood. It is truly a work of God on the heart. God influences the heart of a person by beauty, love, and even adversity to produce forgiveness.

Lewis Smedes wrote that "forgiving is a minor miracle, a bloodless surgery we perform on our spirits. People who discover the grace to forgive almost always discover the grace of hope besides" (*Standing on the Promises* [Nashville: Thomas Nelson Publishers, 1998], p. 108). We need hope in a world in which we find ourselves surrounded by hatred and bloodshed.

For a high school graduation gift my voice teacher gave me Archibald Rutledge's little book *Life's Extras*. Rutledge told about two men who had trouble between them for years. On one occasion they had a fight in town. One of them would have been killed had not someone separated them. He told Archibald, "After that night in town, I figured that one of us would get the other. I knew he always carried a gun, and I began to do the same." Riding his horse up to the other person's lane, intending to end the conflict once and for all, he saw his opponent, Bill Moore, coming toward him.

"I just turned off the road into one of these here baybranches, where I would be hid well. There I sat still on my horse, with the bushes all around me, and with my hand on my gun and the devil in my heart. I put up my left hand to pull aside a little limb, when on it I saw a white flower, a sweet bay flower. And I smelt it, too. My mother used to love that flower; and when I was a boy she made me bring a bush from the swamp and plant it in the yard for her. She was buried with one of them same white flowers in her hand. And, you know, I forgot all about why I had come down that road."

When Bill reached him, he rode out of the bushes. "I didn't want to harm him now. . . . Something in the way I came up made him know it was all right. And it was all right, 'cause we made it right there and then; and we are better friends than ever we were before anything happened. Now what do you think of that—and all because of a . . . little flower?" (*Life's Extras* [New York: Fleming H. Revell, 1928], pp. 17, 18). God used the bay flower—a miracle that triggered forgiveness to replace revenge.

# Chapter 11

# THE PURSUING FORGIVER

The trilogy of stories about the Divine Pursuer found in Luke 15 gives us an intimate look at the Eternal Forgiver. Their beauty is their brevity. It allows each of us to fill in the details with our own imagination. I invite you to personalize these stories in a way that will speak to your own heart and indulge me as *I* fill in some details.

The context of the stories encourages us. People who did not measure up to the standards of the sophisticated clergy of Jesus' day gathered about Him. It was nearly impossible for Him to go anywhere without drawing a crowd. The fact that Jesus treated everybody like old friends upset the religious leaders. Crooked tax collectors, cripples, drunkards, ex-prisoners, the mentally ill—all felt accepted. They listened to Jesus as if their life depended on what He had to say. (And indeed it may have.)

The grumbling of the church bureaucrats as they steadily lost their following to Jesus prompted Him to tell the stories of a sheep, a coin, and a young man. I am especially drawn to the shepherd and the lost sheep because I became a shepherd of sorts at age 14. I pestered my father for permission to buy a pair of sheep until I wore him down. One day he removed the backseat from his

1940 Studebaker Champion before leaving for his job at the city hospital. When he pulled into the barnyard that afternoon I noticed four ears through the car window. I was a shepherd.

After placing them in a stable with clean straw, I sat in the straw until they felt safe enough to eat from a container at my feet. From then on I was not a stranger, but a friend.

Jesus said that a certain shepherd had 100 sheep and one became lost. He searched for it and carried it back to the fold on his shoulders. Then he celebrated with his helpers. For years I pictured the shepherd carrying a gentle lamb on his shoulders, an image probably influenced by the many illustrations I saw of Jesus carrying a lamb. Not until I became a shepherd myself did I realize that the lost sheep could have been the stubborn, belligerent, and rebellious member of the flock.

My buck sheep developed a limp in its front legs. The veterinarian said it had an infection in its feet. He told me to soak the feet in a strong solution three times a day. I isolated the animal in a small pen, sprayed the pen with a strong disinfectant, and built a feed box. Three times a day I straddled the sheep's shoulders to keep it standing in the medication.

One day as I bent over the side of the pen to fill the feed box, the buck struck me on the head with its hard and horned head. I reeled backward against the stable wall and slumped to the floor. For several minutes I could see the stable spinning round and round. After regaining my full consciousness I brought the pan of medication to the pen and soaked my attacker's feet.

Jesus didn't describe the nature of the lost sheep. He simply said the creature was lost. Based on my experience, I can picture the shepherd returning a rascal to the sheepfold. He valued the ornery sheep as much as the 99 compliant ones.

The first lamb born to my pair of sheep nursed frantically all day, but she became thinner and weaker. My mother told me that its mother didn't have adequate milk to help the lamb thrive, so we came up with a plan. I fortified cow's milk with Karo syrup, placed it into a soft drink bottle, and put a nipple on the mouth of the bottle. Three times a day I fed my lamb. Eventually it considered me to be its other mother. It would run to me, settle down on my lap, and drain the bottle dry. The ewe would approach behind me and sniff at my ears. I think it was her way of thanking me for caring for her baby. As a shepherd I learned to care for the gentle, undernourished lamb and the rambunctious buck with equal affection. After all, they were the sheep of my pasture.

Jesus' story is more about the shepherd than about the sheep. He is telling us that God goes in search of those who need to experience the joy of forgiveness. The Shepherd's Psalm concludes: "Surely goodness and lovingkindness will follow me all the days of my life" (Ps. 23:6). Rabbi Harold Kushner says that the word "follow" should be translated "pursue." The Lord is our Pursuing Forgiver. Our personality, background, education, wealth, and lifestyle don't change His love. He is the Good Shepherd who forgives wayward sheep no matter how long or how far they have wandered.

H.M.S. Richards, Sr., was a master storyteller. I heard him tell about a shepherd in the highlands of Scotland. The man's little girl begged to accompany him every day when he went out to care for his sheep. Most of all, she loved to hear her father summon the sheep. He'd cup his hands to his mouth and call. The sound of his voice echoed over the wine-red moors of Scotland.

When his little girl grew into womanhood, she decided to go to Edinburgh for education and employment. Her father accompanied her on the train. As he boarded the train for the trip home his daughter promised to write.

Every week he eagerly read her letters. But gradually their frequency dwindled and then stopped. A friend told the shepherd that it could be a bad omen. The old man's heart ached. He decided he *must* go to Edinburgh and find her. Having no idea where she might be in that large city, he walked through the streets with his hands cupped to his mouth giving the shepherd's call. Far into the night he searched.

The daughter sat in a house of ill repute. Faintly she heard the shepherd's call. Not another shepherd in the whole world had a call like that. It must be her father. Her eyes brightened. Leaving the house, she followed the sound of the familiar voice. In minutes she was in the arms of her shepherd father. He took her home and nursed her back to decency.

Our God tramped the streets of our world in the nadir of its history, giving the call to forgiveness. When we fall into His embrace, we go from spiritual poverty to heavenly riches. Instead of being filled with bitterness, resentment, and hatred, we now experience forgivenness and forgivingness.

A woman lived in a simple Galilean home. An assortment of crudely woven grass mats covered the dirt floor. Although tiny windows let in small shafts of light, she still had to keep a lamp constantly burning to see in the house.

For some reason she kept 10 treasured silver coins in an earthen pot. Regularly she dumped them on her kitchen table, polished them, counted them, and returned them to the pot for safekeeping. One cloudy day when she emptied them onto the table, a coin rolled to the floor without her noticing. Before she realized it, she had walked back and forth across the floor while she polished the coins. When she counted them as she returned them to the pot, she found only nine. One was missing.

Quickly she glanced at the floor, but she could not see it. Picking up the lamp from the table, she grabbed her broom. After sweeping most of the floor she saw the coin. It was dusty, dirty, and trampled upon. That did not matter because she knew that the dirt would wash off. Her coin was still silver inside.

She held the coin close to her heart and ran outside. Her neighbors heard her happy voice calling, "Come to my house. I'm throwing a big party. I found my coin!" The woman had returned her coin to the community of shiny silver.

A young woman in a psychiatric ward was feeling dusty, dirty, and trampled upon. She had tried to end her life. Now she was certain that God could not forgive her. I told her Jesus' parable of the lost coin.

"Where did you find that story?" she asked.

"In an ancient book I have at home," I replied.

"I love that story. Would you tell me that story every day?"

After I had related it to her for more than a week, she said, "Chaplain, thank you for telling me the story. You don't have to repeat it anymore. I know I am still silver." She knew that in spite of her actions God saw the silver—that she had been forgiven.

A young soldier just returned from the war in Iraq was my seatmate on a flight from Chicago to Lansing, Michigan. He hooked his seat belt, heaved a sigh, and said, "Sir, I just came back from a one-year tour in Iraq. My platoon touched down in Texas where we had our debriefing. It was raining cats and dogs, but I stood on the tarmac, looked up to the sky, and let the rain soak my khakis. After a year in desert dust I was ready for rain."

We were quiet during most of the flight. Several times I noticed him slapping his knees and laughing quietly to himself. As the pilot prepared to land he said, "Sir, you might think it strange to be laughing. You see, I'm so happy to be going home that I'm beside myself. My wife is expecting me tomorrow, but I got away early to surprise her."

My soldier seatmate had home in his heart. I identified with him because I left home at 16 to attend a boarding school in Philadelphia. Every other Friday afternoon I walked to the road leading to home. There I stuck out my thumb and hoped for a ride. Even though I didn't have a winter coat or gloves, I would still hitchhike in the winter cold. It didn't matter that I was cold because I had home in my heart. As dozens of cars whizzed by without stopping, I thought of Mom's cooking, especially her shoo-fly pie. Thoughts of home gave me courage.

Home—nothing could erase memories of it from the heart of the young prodigal in Jesus' story. Jesus didn't say why he left home. Perhaps the son wanted to be free from his father's rules, or maybe it was a surge of the independent spirit that sweeps over so many young men.

I get the feeling that the father wasn't pleased about the son's decision, but he didn't stand in his way. Sadly, he handed him his share of the inheritance. Maybe he figured that his son would have to learn the hard way.

With no regard for his father's feelings, the son headed for the bright lights and the fast pace. What he thought would be freedom turned out to be bondage. Fair-weather friends went in search of other country bumpkins when his money ran out. His fascination with fancy women and gaudy clothes ended when his stomach went empty for days.

A famine struck where he was living. He had no reserves and no friends. Finally he managed to meet a pig farmer who took him in, but he received only a starvation diet as pay. Even the pig slop looked appetizing at times. Every night he went to sleep hungry. And as he sat by the pigpen, half starved, he thought again about his parents' love and generous provisions. Thoughts of home overwhelmed him like a sudden gale-force wind.

One thing this rebel didn't do was speak of his father unkindly. In positive and complimentary words he said, "All those farmhands working for my father sit down to three meals a day, and here I am starving to death. I'm going back to my father" (Luke 15:17, Message). The young man hit the road with just the clothes on his back and the smell of swine in his nostrils.

As he thought about his father's wealth he acknowledged his own poverty. Also he remembered his father's generosity and the love that he had experienced during his growing up years. Filled with sorrow for having left home, he prepared a little speech to make to his father. He didn't doubt his father's forgiveness. Maybe the speech was a way of handling his nervousness.

Ambling down the road, his thoughts of home became clearer. He could already taste his mother's falafels and pita bread. The faces of his parents and the farmhands sitting around the dining room table flashed across his mind. The wayward boy was already home because home was in his heart.

A poem written by Roger Altman has always colored my impression of the father. The leader of an adult church class asked me to memorize the poem and recite it. The poet pictured the father sitting on the front porch smelling the wisteria blooms on the trellis next to the porch. He was watching for his son day after day. One day he sees someone coming down the path. At first he wonders who it could be, because age has dimmed his eyesight, but he concludes that it is his son. His son has come home.

I don't believe the father rocked on the front porch day after day. The trilogy of Luke 15 portrays a woman methodically sweeping the floor to find her coin. It pictures a shepherd roaming the hillsides looking for his sheep. Thus it makes sense that the same theme of pursuing would carry over to the story of the lost boy. The Bible says the father met the son a long way from home. He wasn't rocking on the front porch. That forgiving father went in pursuit of his son. Isn't that the natural impulse of a good father?

Our family visited Mackinaw Island in Michigan. We went to the old fort and enjoyed the drum and fife music and the firing of the large cannon. As we toured one of the historic homes we suddenly realized that our granddaughter was not with us. In a flash every one of us scattered throughout the house and into the yard. Waiting for a 3-year-old to find her family is folly and dangerous. Pursuing her, we found her chatting with a perfect stranger.

As weeks passed and the father in Jesus' parable didn't hear from the son, he feared the worst. He went to the far country to find his son who needed the comfort and joy of home. Dirty, tired, and sick, the son was stumbling along the roadway when he saw a familiar form accompanied by servants. He knew it was characteristic of his father to look for him. Instantly he began his speech, but the father wasn't listening. He was ordering his servants to put new shoes on his son's feet and a ring on his finger, a sure sign that the father considered him a member of the family. The father slipped a new robe around the boy's shoulders. The servants lifted him onto a donkey, and they made their way home.

In my imagination I hear their conversation as they journey along. The son says, "Father, I know you cut me off before I finished my speech, but I must tell you how sorry I am for causing you so much grief and pain."

"But you never ceased being my son," the father

answers. "You were forgiven the day you left home. Today my heart sings because you have come home to enjoy my forgiveness. We'll have a party when we get home, and our future will be joyous."

Sitting astride the animal, the son is too choked up to respond to such love. He quietly weeps until he is able to haltingly say, "Thank . . . thank . . . thank you . . . Father."

It takes time to kill a fat calf and turn it into barbecue. Preparations for the homecoming feast were not a micro-waved frozen dinner affair. The mother and all the household servants scurried around the farmhouse. Messengers ran to neighbors and welcomed them to the feast. This celebration would last a long time.

When the party was in full swing, the older brother angrily demanded an explanation from the father. The father labored with the son, but that's where the story ends. The younger son is enjoying forgiveness he does not deserve. The older son thinks his hard work should have earned him a party years ago. He doesn't realize that the only way he can resolve his anger and resentment is to accept his father's love as a gift and then pass that gift on to his younger brother.

If you are a younger brother or sister living in the far country of resentment and grudges, you are probably starved for love and intimacy from those you once held dear. But there is a solution. God is right now initiating your return. His forgiveness, the key to handling anger constructively, has been flowing from eternity and will continue to flow. Look full in Jesus' wonderful face. His glory and grace will dim the hostilities of the past and present. Standing in His presence, you will realize that you are a spiritual pauper and that God's forgiveness is priceless. Tap into the deep stream of His forgiveness, and that refreshing forgiveness will also flow out to those who have hurt and offended you.

Life is too short to live in the far country of harbored animosity. You can meet the Pursuing Forgiver and once again enjoy the home of joy and peace.

If you are an older brother or sister, join the party! As my grandmother always reminded me, "Don't cut off your own nose to spite your face." Eugene H. Peterson's paraphrase of Luke 15:31 says, "His father said, Son, you don't understand" (Message). As I read this rendering of the text I thought, *Maybe the father is saying to his resentful son—you don't understand your father.* If we understood God more deeply we would be less able to embrace anger toward others.

It is quite possible that the older brother did work diligently on his father's farm, but he had never fully tasted the joys of being at home. He had never learned to serve without seeking something in return. His anger, resentment, jealousy, and desire for revenge indicate that he had left home while still sleeping in the father's house.

"There are many elder sons and elder daughters who are lost while still at home. And it is this lostness—characterized by judgment and condemnation, anger and resentment, bitterness and jealousy—that is so pernicious and so damaging to the human heart" (Henri J. M. Nouwen, *The Return of the Prodigal Son* [New York: Doubleday, 1992], p. 70).

The thought has crossed my mind that the reason Jesus placed the older brother as well as the younger one in the story is to make us aware that we can be both. At times we are close to God and forgiving and understanding of others. Other times we are not as close to God as we should be, and we become judgmental and ready to take vengeance on those who might offend us.

Henri J. M. Nouwen commented that "both needed healing and forgiveness. Both needed to come home. Both needed the embrace of a forgiving father. But from the story itself . . . it is clear that the hardest conversion to go through is the conversion of the one who stayed home" (*ibid.,* p. 66).

The father approached both sons, but their responses were strikingly different. But that did not change his willingness to forgive. And he went seeking both sons, but only one was willing to be found.

When my grandsons were very small, they loved to play hide and seek. The oldest boy tried to find the most inconspicuous places to hide. The younger boy didn't quite understand the rules of the game. When I came to seek him, he'd make little noises so that I would locate him. But the oldest son in Jesus' story would not be found even when his father came into full view of him.

To me, the most stunning statement that the father made to the oldest son is "Everything I have is yours." Our Pursuing Forgiver holds nothing back. All the power of heaven is at our disposal to forgive those who trespass against us. Everything we need to live a joyful life is free for the asking. Perhaps that is why Jesus has the story of the prodigal son take place in a wealthy family.

Finally, we come to the celebration. The shepherd told his friends and neighbors, "Rejoice with me, for I have found my sheep which was lost!" (Luke 15:6). The woman gathered her friends and said, "Rejoice with me, for I have found the coin which I had lost!" (verse 9). And the father threw a big party because his son was safe at home. The shepherd, the woman, and the father represent God who rejoices over every individual who opens to His forgiveness. All heaven rejoices with Him. I have no idea what a celebration in heaven is like, but there must be many of them going on because every person who accepts free salvation prompts such rejoicing.

You may recall the times when space explorers returned to earth during the early days of the space program. They received heroes' welcomes. The many honors included ticker-tape parades, TV interviews, and visits to the White House. Every young person in America and other parts of the globe aspired to be astronauts. They drew crowds wherever they went.

Imagine what the celebration will be like when all sinners who have accepted God's forgiveness reach their eternal home. There will be no older brothers and sisters. All the resentments and provocations of earth will be over. We will be like Him for we shall see Him as He is—forgiving, thoughtful, peaceful, and kind. All of us will go into the Father's house and celebrate each other's homecoming.

The prophet John got a hint of what that celebration will sound like. "I heard as it were the voice of a great multitude, and as the voice of many waters, and as the voice of mighty thunderings, saying, Alleluia: for the Lord God omnipotent reigneth" (Rev. 19:6, KJV). John portrayed that celebration as the marriage of the Lamb to the finely clothed bride. His word picture of this event is pitifully inadequate, because he just didn't have words to describe it. As we read his description we can only imagine the scene.

I'm not accustomed to big celebrations. The one that stands out in my mind is my graduation from college. I worked my entire way through in five years. I had dreamed of this day for what seemed like an eternity. Now I was marching down the aisle to receive my diploma. Gratitude and joy overwhelmed me, and tears came to my eyes. It was an emotional high.

When I enter the heavenly celebration hall I think I will be overcome with feelings such as I have never had before. Words will fail me. I will stand before the Pursuing Forgiver speechless and weeping for joy. If you are standing next to me, maybe you can sing a song of gratitude to God for me.